"Elisa Morgan understands that the light of the gospel spreads one heart at a time—among preschoolers, among mothers, among others. In *Twinkle*, she calls us beyond excuses to action as witnesses for our Lord Jesus Christ. She also explains how to move from paralysis in sharing our faith to having an eternal impact on the people around us. Honest, warm, practical—*Twinkle* will help you shine. I highly recommend it."

Franklin Graham, president and CEO, Billy Graham Evangelistic Association, Samaritan's Purse

"I have been reading books on evangelism for thirty years. You are now holding the book that will go right near the front of the top shelf. It is personal in the very best sense of that term. There is no religious jargon. There is nothing but honest and sincere wisdom on interacting with today's seekers. It is practical in the best way possible, offering help while acknowledging the genuine complexities of current culture and contemporary people. *Twinkle* is simply one of the most helpful books on evangelism I have ever read. Everyone who reads this book will be better equipped to have a conversation with today's seekers."

Todd Hunter, national director, Alpha USA

"Elisa Morgan has been a high-watt light burner for a whole lot of folks. Your own light will shine a little brighter if you let this book do its work for you."

John Ortberg, teaching pastor, Menlo Park Presbyterian Church

"I love the saying, 'preach the gospel everywhere you go and if necessary . . . use words!' With that in mind, I am impressed with the brilliance of *Twinkle*. Elisa Morgan opens her heart and her life to show how living life authentically and sincerely spreads the light of God to those around us. Her real-life experiences and heartfelt encounters provide a universe of hope to those of us who are not necessarily blessed with the gift of evangelism. Thanks, Elisa, for showing us how our everyday faith can lead to saving faith for those who are watching."

Wess Stafford, president and CEO, Compassion International

"Elisa Morgan's *Twinkle* is one of the most persuasive and essential books on evangelism that I have ever read. Her words remind us that sharing our faith should be compassionate, perceptive, and always feel as natural and warm as flickering light."

Matthew Paul Turner, author of *Provocative Faith* and *The Coffeehouse Gospel*

twinkle

Sharing Your Faith One
Light at a Time

ELISA MORGAN

Grand Rapids, Michigan

Published by Fleming H. Revell
a division of Baker Publishing Group
P.O. Box 6287, Grand Rapids, MI 49516-6287

Printed in the United States of America

Library of Congress Cataloging-in-Publication Data
Morgan, Elisa, 1955–
    Twinkle : sharing your faith one light at a time / Elisa Morgan.
       p.   cm.
    ISBN 0-8007-3062-3 (pbk.)
    1. Witness bearing (Christianity) I. Title.
BV4520.M62 2006
248′.5—dc22   2005027034

Scripture is taken from the HOLY BIBLE, NEW INTERNATIONAL VERSION®. NIV®. (Copyright © 1973, 1978, 1984 by International Bible Society, used by permission of Zondervan) and Today's New International Version™ (Copyright © 2001 by International Bible Society). All rights reserved.

Published in association with the literary agency of Alive Communications, Inc., 7680 Goddard Street, Suite 200, Colorado Springs, CO 80920.

To Ethan

Keep following the star . . .

Contents

Acknowledgments

Every book is the result of many hands and hearts contributing to one author's words. I am so very grateful for the many hands and hearts that invested in bringing *Twinkle* to reality.

The MOPS leaders: Thanks for being so very much like me: concerned about the *I can'ts* of sharing your faith but eager to move to the *I cans* because you love moms who need Jesus.

Jeff Bone, Cyndi Bixler, Cheryl Davis, Beth Flambures, Carla Foote, Carol Kuykendall, Beth Lagerborg, Ethan Morgan, Evan Morgan, Karen Parks, and Constance Smith: Thank you for reading section after section and for your vital input along the way.

Jennifer Leep: Thank you for sharpening your pencil in the form of your mouse and highlighting away at the big and little things that would make *Twinkle* shine more brightly.

Paula Gibson: Thank you for this great cover!

Rick Christian: Thank you for believing in me and in the words God can speak in and through me.

And to all those who have shone their light into my life, I am grateful.

"When people are placed in darkness,
crimes will be committed.
The guilty are not just those who commit the crimes
but those who create the darkness."

Martin Luther King Jr.

"Our deepest fear is not that we are inadequate.
Our deepest fear is that we are powerful beyond measure.
It is our light, not our darkness, that most frightens us.
We ask ourselves, Who am I to be
brilliant, gorgeous, talented and fabulous?
Actually who are you not to be?
You are a child of God.
Your playing small doesn't serve the world.
There is nothing enlightened about shrinking
so that other people won't feel insecure around you."

Nelson Mandela

THIS LITTLE LIGHT OF MINE

"Don't ask for the moon when you have the stars."

Anonymous

I've not really led that many people to Jesus. Maybe three or four directly. If you count family, maybe a couple more. (It depends on the day with teenagers, you know.) I've been to seminary. I lead an international nonprofit with the focus of helping moms of preschoolers come to see the help and hope they can have in Jesus. I write and speak, and yes, I guess there are probably people who've asked Jesus to be in their lives as a result of various talks and sermons I've given over the years.

But personally, in the day to day of life, I don't have a big tally of conversions. The number of individuals who have directly prayed to receive Jesus in my presence is few.

Three or four converted souls hardly qualify me to write a book about sharing faith with others. But conversion isn't really what this book is about.

I have a theory—about the effect of light on darkness.

Not long ago I was looking for a dark place to test my theory. So I grabbed a pack of matches, the ones I use to light my sometimes romantic but always soothing bath candles, and headed into my closet. I shut the door, turned out the light, and peered about in the darkness. Nothing. Darkness is a weird thing. Even if I opened my eyes WIDE, I just couldn't see anything. Zip.

Then I struck a match. Where there had been darkness—impenetrable, dense, and black—there was now light. Suddenly I could make out the contents of my closet. Shoes. Shirts. Laundry on the floor. Under the hanging garments, a pile of stuff to give away. Just as the match started to scorch my fingers, I blew it out. Darkness returned.

Voilá. Just as I suspected. Light changes the very nature of darkness. With the smallest dot of light, images become evident, shapes are revealed. Darkness withdraws in the presence of light.

We live in a dark world. Tsunamis. Terrorists. Hurricanes. Child molestations. Pornography. Both globally and personally, we live in a dark world. I have faced seasons of darkness where I have bumped into unrecognizable objects. Divorce. Alcoholism. Death. Rebellion. Rejection. Infertility. Homosexuality. Unemployment. Cancer. Learning disabilities. Drugs. Tragedy. Legal issues. Transitions. Teen pregnancy. Abuse. Through my own choices or the choices of those I love, darkness has hemmed me in, threatening to snuff out any source of light. In such moments, I'm left to feel my way blindly along walls that seem to lead nowhere.

I need the light of hope. I need to know that I can find my way to someplace less dark. And I'm not alone in this need. You and I are a hope-dependent people. We live in a world that longs for the light of life.

"In the beginning was the Word, and the Word was with God, and the Word was God. He was with God in the beginning. . . . In him was life, and that life was the light of men" (John 1:1–2, 4). Way back in the beginning of everything, God's first act of creation was to bring light into the darkness. "Let there be light," he pronounced in Genesis 1.

Into the darkness, God brought light. And our world has been forever changed. After a long night, morning comes, bringing the sun's rays into our days. Light beckons us into stores and restaurants. It allows us to read and work. It shines over operating tables, enabling a surgeon to repair the wounds of life. It glows in a baby's room at night, promising the safety of love nearby. It illuminates the pavement as our car glides down the freeway, lighting the way home.

Light changes our world. And it changes us. God has brought physical light into our world, and through his Son he brings spiritual light into our lives. And now, we who have this light in us are called to shine his light in such a way that those around us see the light and are drawn to its source. In Philippians 2:14–16, Paul writes to this group of first-century believers, "Do everything without complaining or arguing, so that you may become blameless and pure, children of God without fault in a crooked and depraved generation, in which you shine like stars in the universe as you hold out the word of life."

Get it? What a contrast God's light in us is against the inky blackness of the dark sky! As effortlessly as a star hanging in the night sky, our light makes a difference simply because of what it is: LIGHT! When we shine, we hold out the Word of life to a world in deep need. When we shine, we draw others to the source of our hope. Even a single speck of light alters the very nature of darkness. So . . . twinkle, twinkle, little star! Shine the hope of light into this dark world!

In the face of such a challenge, our knees wobble and our eyes roll back in our heads with a "yeah, right" response. All we can see are the *I can'ts*:

I can't . . . I have such a small light. How could I possibly make a difference?

I can't . . . I might fail. I might mess up at sharing my faith.

I can't . . . I don't want to get involved. Sharing with others is risky and expensive in terms of time and energy.

I can't . . . I don't want to offend. I don't want to stick out in the crowd. Besides, isn't faith a personal thing?

I can't . . . I don't have a dramatic story to tell. It'd be different if I did.

I can't . . . I don't know all the answers. What if someone asks me something about God that I don't know? Besides, isn't this my pastor's job?

I can't . . . I don't know how to relate to people who aren't like me. People don't even believe in the Bible anymore; how are they going to believe me?

Does any human soul feel up to the task of sharing our faith?

And yet, we who have God's light burning within us are asked to share that light with others. All of us. I have this gut conviction that God wouldn't invite us to be a part of something impossible. In my soul, I have a feeling that we make the whole share-your-faith thing much more difficult than God makes it. I have this suspicion that our *I can'ts* won't hold up in real life when we meet a person stuck in a dark and hopeless situation. We can hide behind them, but God's light will poke out of our very beings—if only from our very real human cracks.

This book is about the fact that even a tiny speck of light changes the very nature of darkness. It's about moving from the *I can't* to the *I can* of relational evangelism. It's about shining in the day to day in such a way that we help others move one step closer to Jesus. It's about sharing our faith one light at a time. It's about the difference we can make by twinkling.

This little light of mine, inadequate as it may seem at times, has changed the darkness of our days and has changed the darkness in the lives of those we love.

Open your front door and head down the street in your neighborhood. Notice the mom pushing a stroller, the retiree walking his dog. At a stoplight, look over at the person driving in the car next to you. Watch the shoppers at your local mall. Meet the gaze of the grocery clerk bagging your vegetables. In our dark world, people need light. The light of God in us changes the very nature of darkness. God challenges us to shine like stars in the universe as we hold out the Word of life.

What would that look like for you? What would it mean for you to twinkle?

"Shine like stars in the universe as you hold out the word of life."
....
Philippians 2:15–16

PART ONE

Getting Past the *I Can'ts*

There was once a dark cave, deep down in the ground, underneath the earth and hidden away from view. Because it was so deep in the earth, the light had never been there. The cave had never seen light. The word "light" meant nothing to the cave, who couldn't imagine what "light" might be.

Then one day, the sun sent an invitation to the cave, inviting it to come up and visit.

When the cave came up to visit the sun it was amazed and delighted because the cave had never seen light before, and it was dazzled by the wonder of the experience.

Feeling so grateful to the sun for inviting it to visit, the cave wanted to return the kindness and so it invited the sun to come down to visit it sometime, because the sun had never seen darkness.

So the day came, and the sun came down and was courteously shown into the cave.

As the sun entered the cave, it looked around with great interest, wondering what "darkness" would be like. Then it became puzzled, and asked the cave, "Where is the darkness?"

Source Unknown

I can't . . .

I have such a small light.

I might fail.

I don't want to get involved.

I don't want to offend.

I don't have a dramatic story to tell.

I don't know all the answers.

I don't know how to relate to people who aren't like me.

"A saint
   is someone
   who
   lets light shine
through them,
      like
         a
   stained glass window."

Robert Gelinas

I used to listen to a radio preacher on my way in to work each day. Morning after morning he would tell stories of conversations he'd had with people who were "on their way" to Jesus. On planes. In checkout lines. One day he even shared how his doctor had voiced an interest in knowing Jesus, and while stripped down to his skivvies on the examination table, the evangelist had told him how he could know God.

The guy amazed me, intimidated me, and to be honest, kind of ticked me off. I felt so inadequate in comparison. He's a floodlight. I'm a penlight. I stumble over what "door-opening" questions could start up such a dialogue. On airplanes I like to read *People* magazine. It's my "five minutes of peace" in my chaotic world. And doctors, whether they're male or female—no way I'm going to talk about Jesus while clad in only a paper sheet. My light is too little!

And yet . . . while I stumble in starting a conversation, once finally started, I manage to keep it going. (Not everyone can accomplish that!) On airplanes, my *People* magazine has grabbed more than one seatmate into a fascinating dialogue on the latest gossip, even leading to deeper issues! As for doctors . . . once dressed and forking over my insurance co-pay, I can actually look them in the eye.

So many of us face this *I can't* in relational evangelism. *I can't . . . I have such a small light!*

Floodlight and penlight. They're different to be sure. But is one *better* than the other in making a difference in a dark world? Do we have to be BIG lights to twinkle?

When we come to know Jesus, his light comes into us. He is the light of the world. He brings his light into the darkness of our less than perfect souls and offers forgiveness and hope. God's light in us, then, becomes his light in our world.

But then God goes a step further. Buried in the Psalms is a verse that underlines God's tender customization of his light in our personalities. "He determines the number of the stars and calls them each by name" (Ps. 147:4). Identifying your kind of light and shining its offering kills the first *I can't*. As there are both strengths and weaknesses in all personalities, so there are both in our expression of God's light to our world. We do well to label our light, to understand its offering, and then to wield it well in lighting the way for others.

What kind of light are you?

Are you a candle? Do you light the room around you? Are you vulnerable to other influences that might snuff you out?

How about a flashlight? Do you click on in emergencies? Are you good at shining in a pinch but turn off in the everyday?

Are you a desk lamp? Do you provide light for people to work by but need to be atop a steady surface to do so?

Maybe you're a headlight. You light the path for a journey, but you have to be moving in order to not run your battery down.

Could you be a neon light? Do you shine with an appealing hue, but in your offering, do you make your surroundings look different than they really are?

How about a pilot light? Are you necessary for others to be lit, but when you go off they go off too?

Might you be a searchlight? Shining in order to discover who is lost in the darkness?

Are you a spotlight who makes another more visible than yourself?

Or a stoplight controlling the flow of life around you?

Think about a lantern. Do you light your surroundings with a gradual glow?

You might be a sunlamp. Do you provide color to the mundane of life at the risk of danger?

Are you a taillight? Visible only when exiting?

How about a flare? Are you short-lived, rising up only to signal danger or to call for help?

Might you be a chandelier? Do you reflect light from your many facets to illuminate the room around you?

Or a lighthouse? Do you provide light as a direction into a safe harbor?

Are you a glowworm or a lightning bug?

A firecracker or a rocket?

Floodlight or penlight?

What kind of light are you?

We discover great freedom in understanding and accepting our own light "container." Freedom to be me instead of you or you instead of me. Because each light presents a customized offering, contained within the strengths and weaknesses of our individual personalities. They exhibit Jesus uniquely to our world and work best in specific situations.

Floodlights are terrific for shining light on an actor on the stage so that even the last row of the audience can see, but they are not so great for the flash on a camera. While my radio preacher friend's floodlight may show others the way to God, it might "blind" some of the shyer types. Penlights are perfect for reading a ticket stub in a theater but are less than helpful in flagging down help when stranded on a dark roadside. My penlight offering may be too weak for some souls to notice, but it can attract quieter souls to the hope they might not even have recognized they need.

When labeled and lit, our lights can offer just the right light to meet someone else's need for light in a dark place.

Admittedly, there are days when even after labeling our light, we still wonder how successful we'll be in helping others hope. On those days our light is not just little—it's dim. Life eats away at our confidence, our stamina, even at our own conviction of hope. We all experience dark seasons where we can barely light the next step for our own foot. And we wonder how we can light the way for another caught up in a storm.

In such moments, we're helped when we remember that even the dimmest light is brighter than darkness. A little bit of light makes a big difference.

In the aftermath of one of the Florida hurricanes, people from all over the country enlisted to help. One woman took it as her passion to provide flashlights for the children who were left without electricity. Worried that they would be afraid in the darkness, she rallied her forces to provide a flashlight for every child. She knew the loneliness and fear brought on by darkness. And she determined that she would bring light to those who so desperately needed it. She conquered one giant *I can't . . . I have such a small light.* By labeling her light as a flashlight, she brought hope into the hands of those stuck in the darkness.

God is light. He places his light in us that we may have hope for ourselves and hope to share with others. So label your light and hold it up bravely so that others may see and follow after its glow.

"He determines the number of the stars and calls them each by name."
. . . .
Psalm 147:4

I can't . . .

I have such a small light.

I might fail.

I don't want to get involved.

I don't want to offend.

I don't have a dramatic story to tell.

I don't know all the answers.

I don't know how to relate to people
who aren't like me.

"O thou great Chief,
light a candle in my heart,
that I may see what is therein,
and sweep
 the rubbish
from thy dwelling place."

African schoolgirl

Year after year, I look forward to the ceremony of light on Christmas Eve. It's always the same. Light coming into darkness. Drama. Beauty. Power. In the twilight, someone strikes a match. An arm stretches the match to a lone candle. Its wick catches flame. The candle reveals the face of its holder as she holds out her candle to others around her. One by one, around the sanctuary, unlit candles bow to flames, licking the light and making it their own. *Silent night. Holy night. All is calm. All is bright.* The glow grows across the church pews until the space is lit with light.

Beginning with the pastor up on the platform and radiating out to the congregation, light travels to human hearts. Perhaps the most stunning reality of this light liturgy is that I am invited to participate. I stand in my pew—one year huddled with my husband, balancing a toddler on my hip . . . in another year, patting a restless eight-year-old . . . in another, glancing at my apathetic teen. I bow my unlit candle to the soft blaze of a neighboring wick, and its flame ignites, bringing light to the spot beneath my nose. My very own light in the darkness.

It could be that I wouldn't have such an opportunity. It could be that only the pastor or the priest would light a Christmas candle and hold it out in the darkness for others to see. The beauty of evangelism—of sharing our faith with others—is that *we get to participate.*

God invites us into the process of extending hope to others. He puts his light in the containers of our personalities and asks us to hold it out that people might see him and bring their unlit life to him for hope. We get to offer a candle of his hope to others.

I catch my breath. Don't puff so! The flame will go out! Careful! The hot wax burns as it drips over the paper guard and scorches the soft skin between my thumb and index finger. Oooh! Watch out for that little girl's hair in front of me! Now, hold it high—watch it glow! See how it lights the room around me—my own little light!

A candle on Christmas Eve is such a terrible, wonderful, delightful, fearful thing to hold. Yes, we get to participate, but what if we mess up? And here is the reality of the second *I can't* of relational evangelism. *I can't . . . I might fail.* I might come on too strong. I might say the wrong thing. I might push someone away from Jesus. I might blow it—or worse—my candle might BLOW OUT before the person next to me gets to light her candle from it!

Sitting in my Christmas Eve pew, I watch the light as it begins in the darkness. Match strikes. Wick lights. Candles pass. Light comes into the darkness. And I realize something. The origination of light has nothing to do with me. It's beyond my reach or power or control. Light coming into darkness is an act of God just as Jesus coming to our earth is his gift to humankind.

My candle is my personal participation. It's my role. My part. My little bit of the life-changing light. I am not responsible for light coming into the world. That is God's territory. But I am responsible for my candle. I bow it toward God's flame. I cup its fragile flame against the breezes of life around me. I hold it high that others might make their way by its glow. I join the crowd of flames that stretch their pointed tips like star beams to the ceiling of the sanctuary, lighting the world within the hall of worship and, through the skylights, offering light to the world beyond.

The apostle Paul uses a gardening metaphor to make this same point: "I planted the seed, Apollos watered it, but God has been making it grow. So neither the one who plants nor the one who waters is anything, but only God, who makes things grow" (1 Cor. 3:6–7). Unpacking these verses reveals two basic areas of responsibility in evangelism: God's and ours.

God's part is clear: God is responsible for light. He is light. By his act of creation, he brought light and truth and hope into our world through his Son, Jesus. Miraculously, he makes sense out of what is seemingly senseless. He offers purpose to the inconsequential. He brings light into darkness. He originates light and holds it out to others through us.

Our part? We're responsible for our candles, to keep them lit, burning, visible, available for others.

Whew. Truly, what a relief!

I talked with my friend Janis about this. Her neighbor is looking for light but is kind of picky about where she thinks she'll find it. Janis shines, bright and furious in some moments, tender and quiet in others. Toni watches and concludes, "Well, that faith stuff is nice—for *you*."

So Janis looks down at her flame and wonders, "What's the matter with this thing? Is it too small? Too wimpy? Too bright? What's the deal?" She concludes that her flame looks okay to her, but she's still bothered by a prickly worry. Where is she messing up? What more could she do? Should she pray more often? What about fasting—would that make a difference? What book could she take to Toni? Is her neighbor's lack of response somehow *Janis'* responsibility? Can't Toni make out light in the darkness?

God is responsible for the light. He draws others out of their darkness into his light. Through his Holy Spirit, he attracts them to his flame. We might be the ones holding that flame at the moment, in our shaky and sweaty hands, but the flame remains his. We're not responsible for the origination of light in ourselves or in others.

We're responsible for our candles.

While we can't mess up God's light, we can improve at our candle holding. Here's how:

Trim your wick. When wicks grow too long, charred and used, their flames can curl, flicker, and even go out. Trim your wick often by remembering what you're responsible for in the process of sharing your faith and by refusing to take on a role you've not been given: God's. Or as you sit in the dark of doubting moments, remembering what you wish you'd said to a friend earlier, release your self-punishment and just determine to speak up the next time you get the chance. Keep a short wick in terms of how much responsibility you take for evangelism and how much you beat yourself up for not doing it "right."

Shield your flame. The forces of life around us will surely threaten your flame. Sickness. Suffering. Death. Depression. Disappointment. Gather your flame next to the flames of others so that your glow might increase. Cup your flame and allow the company of a crowd of other believers to protect it in challenging times.

Hold it high. When we wonder if our flame matters, it's easy to let our arm drop and give up on its value. Resist this urge. Instead, extend your elbow and hold your flame high. Above the crowd, your flame is more visible than buried beneath the hunched shoulders of others.

I can't . . . I might fail is a real concern. But when we tease apart our responsibility from God's role in evangelism, the risk is smaller, and the process is doable. God is responsible for light. We're responsible for our candles. Did you get that? We're responsible for our *can*dles!

"I planted the seed, Apollos watered it, but God has been making it grow."
. . . .
1 Corinthians 3:6

I have such a small light.

I might fail.

I can't . . . **I don't want to get involved.**

I don't want to offend.

I don't have a dramatic story to tell.

I don't know all the answers.

I don't know how to relate to people
who aren't like me.

"Somebody has to go polish the stars.
They're looking a little bit dull."

Shel Silverstein

They lived next door to us for about three years. Giant truck with big tires in the driveway. SUV next to that. Camper on the side of the house. Then there was the landscaping, or lack thereof. A patch of gravel dotted with weeds. The paint peeled from their gutters. One curtain hung crooked in their side window—as it had since we moved in years prior.

They just didn't seem to care. Or maybe they didn't notice. Whichever it was, the condition of their house bugged me big.

Their kids bugged me too. And it wasn't just that Evan and I didn't have any children yet (you know that lofty spot of childlessness from which it's so easy to evaluate everyone else's parenting skills and prescribe what needs to be added and subtracted Super Nanny style). It was that their children were a bit hoodlummy. They ran around half-clothed in the summer, in and out of the sprinkler that their parents forgot about and left on for hours once they went inside. In the winter they mounded snow into uneven snowmen, leaving their mittens and boots scattered in piles once the snow people melted. Their hair was usually uncombed, stringy, and knotted. Their faces were smeared with the leftovers of whatever they'd consumed at the last meal.

But they were nice enough. I have to give them that. The Carters— mom, dad, and two children—were nice enough people when I had occasion to visit. Something I avoided as often as possible.

One Saturday afternoon I was planting petunias out front when Janet (Mrs. Carter) approached me. My heart hitched it up a step. I rose from my knees and patted my garden-gloved hands to shake off the dirt. On Janet's face was a sweet but shy smile.

"Elisa, I'm sorry to interrupt you—oh, those flowers are lovely!" Well, at least she knew a nice flower when she saw one. "Listen, Rusty [Mr. Carter] and I were wondering if you and Evan would be interested in attending a special program our church is sponsoring. It's on communication and marriage and stuff."

I dropped my trowel right there in the grass. "Er . . . um . . . I didn't know you and Rusty went to church," I stammered. Their garage door had remained solidly shut every Sunday morning when Evan and I had pulled out of our cul-de-sac. What was this?

"Well, we went through some really hard times in our marriage this winter, and we decided to find a church to help us out. We're members now—it's great. In fact, we both became Christians. Anyway, we wondered if you'd be interested."

There I stood in my suburban front yard, receiving an invitation to explore God in church from a woman, a neighbor, who'd come to Christ *in spite* of me. *With no help whatsoever* from me.

I stared through Janet's smile and saw an unavoidable *I can't* regarding relational evangelism that I'd never before acknowledged in myself. But it was true: *I can't . . . I don't want to get involved.* It held me back from sharing my faith with the Carters. In fact, it held me back from even noticing, behind the disarray of their home's outside, that inside they were eager for the help and hope of Jesus. All I'd seen were the weeds and the crooked curtain, and the mitten left in the snow.

Somehow, I bumbled about with an explanation that Evan and I were Christians too, much to her surprise, I'm ashamed to say. She didn't have a clue. Not long after this conversation with Janet, God's Word grabbed my heart and hammered home a truth I can't seem to forget.

The story takes place in Acts 10 and then is driven home in Acts 11. The apostle Peter was in a season of miraculous preaching and powerful proclamation regarding the power of Jesus' resurrection. After Peter's blunder of denials when Jesus was arrested and his later restoration after

Jesus' resurrection, surely this was a man affected by God and effective for him. Except that in Acts 10 we find that he was a bit of a snob toward those who weren't Jews. Peter cared very much about doing his faith "right" and reaching Jews with news of the Messiah: Jesus.

Peter fell into a trance where God revealed that he had also chosen Gentiles for salvation. Peter then received visitors from a God-fearing centurion Gentile named Cornelius who wanted to believe. With these words as his explanation, "Who was I to think that I could oppose God?" (Acts 11:17), Peter shared the gospel with Cornelius and his whole household. News went out to all the apostles that the Gentiles had received the Word of God.

Peter was bugged about associating with those who ate "unclean animals" and so never dreamed that God would be interested in using Peter to bring Gentiles to himself. I was bugged about weeds in gravel and sprinklers left on and so never considered that my light—or rather God's light in me—might be a ray of hope to a family in need. I didn't want to get involved, so I didn't. And consequently, God used somebody else, another light, to bring that family whom he loved to himself. I opposed them. And so God bypassed me.

I'm not proud of this. No way. But now, twenty years later, I also don't think it's healthy to beat myself up for it anymore. Lots and lots of us pull back from folks around us—those who seem to live like us and those who clearly don't. We assume they wouldn't be interested in what we have in Jesus. My neighbors shot down that assumption in defeat and taught me a lesson I still hold in my heart. When I don't want to get involved . . . because someone seems like too much energy, too much work, too deep of a commitment, I try to honestly admit these feelings and tell God about them. I know that in the end, it is his job to bring people to faith, not mine. I can mess up all day, and God can still bring them along. But when I believe the *I can't . . . I don't want to get involved*, I now realize that I'm the one who's missing out. Missing out on an opportunity to watch God work in spite of me.

There. Enough said. An ugly chapter in my life that God redeemed for his purposes.

Is there such a spot in your life? Look around your neighborhood, or just take a stick and stir about in your heart. Is there an *I can't . . . I don't want to get involved* lurking somewhere near the surface? Who are you opposing coming to Christ?

"Who was I to think that I could oppose God?"
....
Acts 11:17

I have such a small light.

I might fail.

I don't want to get involved.

I can't . . . **I don't want to offend.**

I don't have a dramatic story to tell.

I don't know all the answers.

I don't know how to relate to people
who aren't like me.

"I have lived
among the stars
for too long
to fear the night."

American astronomer

W hen my daughter, Eva, was in kindergarten, I began praying for her teacher. Seriously. I wanted her to know the Jesus I loved. I sent her cards in which I underlined our partnership in my daughter's life. I gave her a special Christmas gift. One day in January, halfway through the year of kindergarten, I volunteered in the computer lab with the kids. Me. Computer lab. Kids. It was a stretch, but like I said, I really wanted this lady to know Jesus.

In the middle of a row of Macs, she mentioned that she'd heard I'd written a book and asked where she could buy it. Quickly I told her that I'd be happy to give her a copy. I didn't want to tell her that she could probably only find my book in a Christian bookstore. That would be too "out there" for my quiet sharing. "Let me have Eva bring you a copy. It'll be my gift to you!" I offered.

She scrunched up her face and said, "Hmmm. Mrs. Morgan, I don't know. I really wanted to go get a copy tonight so that I can use it in a Bible study I'm teaching."

A BBBBBBBible study? You're teaching a BBBBBBBible study? I dropped my mouth in surprise. Blinded by her blaze, I stumbled to my next response. "Mrs. Burnett, you must be a Christian," to which she responded, "Absolutely!"

"Did you know that over the Christmas holidays Eva asked Jesus into her heart?" I asked.

"Really?" she squealed. Then she spun Eva around from the computer screen, gently grabbed her shoulders, and looked deep into my daughter's eyes as she exclaimed, "Eva, that makes us special sisters, you and me!"

I stood—dazed—in the computer lab of my child's public school, like Paul on the road to Damascus. I'd been trying to shine in tiny little sparks. Mrs. Burnett turned her light on the room like an extraterrestrial being landing in a sci-fi movie.

I incarnate the *I can't . . . I don't want to offend* posture in relational evangelism.

What is it, exactly, that I'm so worried about? On one side of the issue, I'm concerned that I'll invade someone's personal faith territory. There are gobs of folks out there who've been wounded by us Christians. I sure don't want to add to the pile. After all, faith is a private thing, isn't it?

Yeah, there's that side. But there's also another aspect to this *I can't*. I'm also worried about being rejected. Misunderstood. Looking stupid. I don't want to offend another, and I don't want to be offended myself.

Like the time after college when my boyfriend of six years and I broke up. We'd been on the doorstep of marriage but looked into our future far enough to see that wasn't the direction for us. So we broke up. And I decided to go to seminary to pursue a ministry career. I called my father to tell him. "Elisa," he pleaded through the phone, "don't give up on men! There are a lot of other ones out there." From dabbling in Catholicism, he'd concluded that I was entering a convent to become a nun. Quite a leap. And he's not the only one who has assumed that because I attended seminary I must be some kind of zealot. In various instances I have to "undo" people's understandings of what it means to be a woman and a Christian, and a seminary graduate.

Someone said, "There can be no such thing as secret discipleship, for either secrecy destroys the disciple or discipleship destroys the secret." I think this is what Jesus meant in Luke 8:16 when he explained that the very nature of light is to be revealed, not hidden: "No one lights a lamp and hides it in a clay jar or puts it under a bed. Instead, they put it on a stand, so that those who come in can see the light."

In Jesus' day, the houses in Palestine were very dark inside with only one window, usually circular and about eighteen inches in diameter.

Inside the house, the lamp was the chief source of light, day and night. It stood on a stand, bringing its glow up to eye level, but was covered with an earthen bushel, or bowl, when the homeowners were out so that it would continue to burn without risk. Because it was very hard to kindle a lamp in the first place—flint, tinder, and so on—folks wanted to avoid the hassle of rekindling a lamp if it happened to go out.

But no way was the cover kept on the light when the homeowners were home. How could they see?

The purpose of light is to shine. Not to be hidden. In this passage about light, Jesus goes on to say, "For there is nothing hidden that will not be disclosed, and nothing concealed that will not be known or brought out into the open" (Luke 8:17). When we try to hide our faith, our light, it's like sticking a bowl over it. We can't see where we're going and what we're doing, much less shine in a way that others can see our source of hope and help.

I've had to come to grips with one specific question regarding the light in my life. Am I trying to illuminate light, or am I eliminating it?

Besides Mrs. Burnett and my very good intentions, how else might I be eliminating rather than illuminating—holding tight to the *I can't . . . I don't want to offend* posture? How about you?

I hide my Bible when in public. Like when I hit Starbucks and plop down for some time with God, I keep a magazine around it. It bugs me when people look at me reading the Bible in public. I imagine them cataloging my characteristics: interesting hair, I wonder who does it, but ooohhh, she's reading the BIBLE. Weird. I don't want to worry about who's thinking I'm weird while I'm reading the Bible at Starbucks.

Or . . . I don't want to put one of those fish/dove/etc. symbols on my car's back bumper. I imagine myself questioning my performance on every turn, lane change, and U-turn—not to mention the honks that slip out at slow movers in front of me when the light turns green.

Or . . . I'm on a plane. My seatmate turns to me and asks, "What do you do?" Instead of saying I work for a Christian organization that brings hope to moms of preschoolers, I blurt out, "I work for an international nonprofit that supports moms of preschoolers." Much more culturally aware. Much cooler.

Now hear me carefully, these less-than-revealing responses *can* be appropriate in some circumstances. Like when I'm trying to open the door to discussion. Then they can actually be the launching point of a deeper conversation.

"An international nonprofit for moms of preschoolers? Why do they need support?" the question comes. Then I can respond, "Spend thirty seconds with the mom four rows back who's trying to keep her three-year-old entertained and her infant's ears from popping in the altitude changes and you'll know. Moms are humbled by the gargantuan task of raising the next generation. They need hope. And they need to know they're not alone. The organization I work for believes that Jesus can help moms be the best moms they can be: the influencer of her family and her world."

I've just moved from what could eliminate the light to illuminating it.

We all face such a choice. Eliminate or illuminate. Hide and seek or show and tell. There are certainly instances when a tiny twinkle lights the way home better than a floodlight. But no light versus some light is a different matter altogether. When we eliminate the light, we betray our very being and the presence of God within us. Like Peter in the courtyard during Jesus' trial, we holler, "I never knew him!" all the while wearing a cross around our neck.

So, what's it going to be? Eliminate or illuminate? Hide it under a bushel? No! I'm gonna let it shine!

"No one lights a lamp and hides it in a clay jar or puts it under a bed. Instead,

they put it on a stand, so that those who come in can see the light."
. . . .
Luke 8:16

I have such a small light.

I might fail.

I don't want to get involved.

I don't want to offend.

I can't . . . **I don't have a dramatic story
to tell.**

I don't know all the answers.

I don't know how to relate to people
who aren't like me.

"The stories people
tell have a way of
taking care of them.
If stories come to you,
care for them.
And learn to give
them away where they
are needed. Sometimes
a person needs a story
more than food to
stay alive."

Barry Lopez

Once upon a time. That's how the stories of my childhood began. I loved tales of princesses and dragons and knights and warriors. I loved imaginative folklore with hobbits and worlds-entered-through-wardrobes. But I've also always loved biographies.

In our summer library bookmobile (how ancient is that?), I'd plop down in the corner where real-life stories were shelved and pick my way through until I'd read them all. Hans Christian Andersen, the fairy-tale writer himself. Betsy Ross, seamstress for America's star-spangled banner. Clara Barton, founder of the Red Cross. Thomas Edison, inventor of the lightbulb (among other things). Liliuokalani, Queen of Hawaii. Harriet Beecher Stowe, author of *Uncle Tom's Cabin*. I'd crack open a book and meet a new *friend*.

It wasn't that I was some lonely sort. I had other in-the-flesh friends. It's just that I loved reading stories of *real people*. What made them tick, their fears and dreams and darings, their family foibles and joys, and their hopes. I learned from their lives things that might fit in my life.

Twinkling, shining the light of God's love from our lives into the lives of others, is tied to telling your story about knowing God and the difference Jesus has made to you.

I can't . . . I don't have a dramatic story to tell. You don't have one? Oh, yes you do. Oh, yes you do! Okay, maybe you aren't a hooker who found Jesus at the end of a heroin needle. Maybe you are. Or maybe you didn't convert to Christianity from another world religion after seeing an image of Jesus in your coffee creamer. Maybe you did. Or maybe you used to be depressed and frustrated with your life and you looked into God and eventually got connected to him through Jesus.

I think we need to rethink drama here. Every single story has some element of drama in it. Good versus evil. Struggle to be settled. Riddle to resolve. Mystery to be revealed. And for those of us who've journeyed from death to life in terms of not knowing God through Jesus and then coming to know him—being *saved from death by him*—the drama is undeniable. Though sometimes it's somewhat hidden, or just forgotten.

Stories don't have to be *dramatic* as in made-for-TV dramatic in order to be important as stories. There are all kinds of literature: fiction and nonfiction, biographies and autobiographies, fantasies and folktales. Two parameters guide our story-telling. It must be true and it must be personal. So that leaves out fantasy and fiction.

All stories have several common elements. Besides a beginning, a middle, and an end, they involve a person who faces a problem or a conflict or has a need and then goes through a change that somehow resolves the issue. Not fixes it—resolves it. In a faith story, the change is in the person rather than in the circumstances surrounding the conflict. A faith story, then, focuses on how we faced a situation and the difference God made in our lives and in our ability to cope with that situation today.

Within a faith story, but not always included in every telling, is a testimony that connects your own personal story to the larger story of God's work with humankind. Here is where we can integrate our beliefs (what we know that we know that we know) into the context of our own life journey. When we're first getting to know someone, we might choose to tell our story without our testimony. For example, I might begin with the fact that I grew up in a single-parent home, that my mom struggled with alcohol, and that as a result, I felt the gaps of some heart holes early on in my life. Later in high school, I made sense of some of this pain and found hope and even healing. That's it. There's no direct mention of

Jesus, just a clear description of my need for him and what knowing him brought about in my life.

Admittedly, storytelling comes easier to some than to others. The drama queen launches into her history at the first question. The quieter, more bookish individual may hesitate. We all get better at storytelling with practice.

Here are some suggestions for would-be storytellers of all types:

Ask a good friend to interview you regarding your journey to Jesus and then tape-record your conversation. When you listen back, you may discover insights and phrases worth repeating. At the same time, be on guard for any "Christianese" phrases that won't communicate to someone who doesn't know God and, in fact, that you don't even understand yourself.

Start with a spiritual autobiographical approach. What was your childhood like? What role did God play in your life? Did you go to church? Did you have any spiritual beliefs? Then move on. When do you first remember Jesus, God, or a Christian friend having an impact on you? What was your response? When did spiritual truths first make sense to you? What changed you from thinking Jesus wasn't important to thinking he was real? Were there any personal, family, or life crises around your coming to faith? You get the drift.

Still stuck? Try answering several key questions to get you going. How does God's truth apply to your life today? What difference has knowing Jesus made in your parenting? In your career? In your relationship with your parents? In your relationships with the opposite sex? Which one of God's promises helps you cope in the day to day of life? How has your faith helped you manage a struggle—like a bad habit, a chronic illness, a large life disappointment, your emotions?

Perhaps you need to dig deeper. Select one problem in your life: overeating, worrying, your temper. Describe how you used to handle this matter before you had Jesus in your life compared to now. A word of focus: faith doesn't erase our struggles. They may well still be present. But knowing God through Jesus does adjust our attitude, our goals, and our approach.

Avoid fictionalizing and fantasy making. Don't be afraid to be honest. God can use even the less-than-lovely elements of your upbringing and choice making in lighting the way for others. And don't feel like you have to answer every question about Christianity. You can't.

Face any crossroads you come to and make a decision. There are times when self-examination and spiritual history taking might reveal that we actually don't know Jesus. Yet. What will you do with the revelation? It's easy to believe that you don't have a *dramatic* story to tell when the fact is that you don't really have a story to tell at all. You haven't yet experienced the change that knowing Jesus can make in your life. It's not too late. You can decide right now to respond to God's invitation to begin a relationship by admitting your need for him, asking him to forgive your sin, and surrendering your life to him. How will you respond?

And always pray. Ask God to help you verbalize just what it is he's done in your life. You might put your thoughts down in a journal, share them over coffee with a safe friend, or volunteer to do a devotional in a community gathering. Pick whatever the next "step" is for your storytelling skills and take it.

Peter wrote to first-century believers in Jesus Christ, underlining their change of identity due to their relationship with Christ: "But you are a chosen people, a royal priesthood, a holy nation, a people belonging to God, that you may declare the praises of him who called you out of darkness into his wonderful light" (1 Peter 2:9). Our stories tell others how we got there: out of the darkness into his wonderful light. They move past the *I can't . . . I don't have a dramatic story to tell*, and instead, they declare!

So, what's your story?

"But you are a chosen people, a royal priesthood, a holy nation, a people belonging to God, that you may declare the praises of him who called you out of darkness into his wonderful light."

....

1 Peter 2:9

I have such a small light.

I might fail.

I don't want to get involved.

I don't want to offend.

I don't have a dramatic story to tell.

I can't . . . **I don't know all the answers.**

I don't know how to relate to people
who aren't like me.

"The goofy thing about
Christian Faith
is that you believe it
and don't believe it
at the same time.
It isn't unlike having
an imaginary friend."

Donald Miller

There are moments in life when I just go green. It's all I can do to swallow. Too much information?

Frank sat across from me, his entire demeanor poised to pounce. We were talking about salvation. How it happens. Whether we come to God because he draws us and has determined ahead of time that we'll believe or whether we come out of our own choice. Frank loves to get out his Bible and trap me between chapters and verses. Frank has very specific opinions about this subject. Frank has very specific opinions about most subjects. I do too. Well, sort of.

I have very specific opinions about some parts of the Christian faith—the parts I think are clear and provable and undeniable. But I have friends who have strong opinions about things they think are undeniable that I don't.

Sitting across from Frank, I went green. As far as I'm concerned, this isn't the "fun" part of shining. While I know many people who love apologetics, like my husband for instance, for me this is the dirty work of evangelism. It requires thinking. And logic. And making sense.

If you're the cerebral sort, please forgive my inadequacy here. I can just imagine your disappointment, having picked up this book for the explicit purpose of providing others with a Christian apologetic. You'll find helpful references in the "Twinkle Resources" at the end of this book. It ain't going to happen here.

But when we're sharing our story, there comes a time when *our story isn't enough* and we have to connect our lives to something larger, our light to its source, our faith to a system of belief. Getting past the *I can't . . . I don't know all the answers* can be tricky.

Okay. While I get a bit freaked out putting it in words that others can understand, I do know what I believe. I had to figure it out when I was utterly convicted by Peter's command in 1 Peter 3:15, "Always be prepared to give an answer to everyone who asks you to give the reason for the hope that you have." Mercy. Talk about freaked out. String together the words *always . . . be prepared . . . give an answer . . . to everyone*—that's attention getting. You can't just keep reading, you know? And yet, in the next moment, here comes back that *I can't . . . I don't know all the answers* freak-out moment.

In *Blue Like Jazz*, Don Miller reads my mind and puts my feelings on paper:

> I believe in Jesus; I believe He is the Son of God, but every time I sit down to explain this to somebody I feel like a palm reader, like somebody who works at a circus or a kid who is always making things up or somebody at a Star Trek convention who hasn't figured out the show isn't real.

> Until.

> When one of my friends becomes a Christian, which happens about every ten years because I am such a sheep about sharing my faith, the experience is euphoric. I see in their eyes the trueness of the story.[1]

That's me. It's when others decide to believe that I grow more courageous in expressing what I believe. When others believe, I know that what I know is real. I'm even more convinced.

No, I don't know *all* the answers. But here's what I know that I know that I know:

> God loves us and longs to have a relationship with us (John 3:16).
> God is perfect and will not compromise his perfection (Matt. 5:48).

1. Donald Miller, *Blue Like Jazz* (Nashville: Thomas Nelson, 2003), 51.

We all fall short of God's perfection (Rom. 3:23).

The penalty for this imperfection (called sin) is eternal separation from a relationship with God (Rom. 6:23).

God loves us so much that he was willing to offer his perfect Son, Jesus Christ, to pay the penalty for our sins (1 John 4:10).

We must accept God's gift in order to enter into a loving relationship with him (John 1:12).

When we accept God's gift of the loving relationship with his Son (grace), we will live eternally with him beyond death (John 3:16; Rom. 6:23).

God wants us to let his love change us and how we live (Rom. 12:1–3; 2 Cor. 5:17).

God wants to shine his light and hope through our lives to others (Matt. 5:16; 28:19).

These are the beliefs I hold from the Bible because I believe that the Bible is God's Word and is true. Some people don't. In fact, lots of folks don't. When we run into moms and dads and co-workers and teenagers and neighbors who don't know the Bible, haven't ever read it, and don't believe in it, then what?

I like the help provided by my friend Larry Moody, chaplain of the PGA and president of Search Ministries. He identifies three barriers to Christianity.[2]

The first is an emotional barrier. Many people have been hurt in the past by something or someone they see as "religious." They avoid Christianity because they associate it with a negative experience.

You know folks like this. Lila grew up in a home where she was force-fed faith. Once handed a description of what she could believe by her parents, today Lila doubts God even exists. Because the questions were

2. For more on these barriers, go to www.searchnational.org.

asked and answered for her, Lila has never really even considered her own belief system. To do so would feel like losing herself to her parents' mind-set rather than discovering her own.

A second barrier is intellectual. Some people will reject Christianity intellectually, relying on flawed logic or lack of information. Pete can't get over the problem of evil in our world and assigns the blame for all the mess around us to God. A good God would do something. So he chucks Christianity because he hasn't moved past this point in his research or his thinking.

Finally, there's a volitional barrier. Bottom line, some folks just don't want to believe. The reality of sin in all of us separates us from God, and it's more than uncomfortable to sit with our alienation. Sheila would rather medicate her pain in life with unhealthy relationships than face her need for help. Eric prefers to deny his string of broken romances rather than resolve why he cuts off a girlfriend whenever intimacy buds. Janice and Mitch pour their passion into preserving the planet Earth, recycling, and taking care of their bodies and so assuage their awareness of their need for something larger than themselves.

Any of these three barriers can make it tough for others to hear what we're saying we believe about God. But these barriers don't excuse you and me from knowing what we believe. Remember, God is responsible for the light in our world. We are in charge of our own candle.

Not knowing all the answers is an *I can't* that just doesn't stand up in life. Nobody knows all the answers. For that matter, no one even knows all the questions. Perhaps no one can ever really *know* enough to believe. At some point, we know enough to find faith to take us the rest of the way to Jesus.

What do you know that you know that you know about your faith?

"Always be prepared to give an answer to everyone who asks you

to give the reason for the hope that you have."
....
1 Peter 3:15

I have such a small light.

I might fail.

I don't want to get involved.

I don't want to offend.

I don't have a dramatic story to tell.

I don't know all the answers.

I can't . . .   **I don't know how to relate to people who aren't like me.**

"Flame is cleaner seen
if
its container does not compete."

Luci Shaw

Aaron is the lead singer in a Christian rock band. A baseball cap sits cockeyed atop his spiked hair. His jeans are torn with holes, but clean. His T-shirt sports a graffiti-like scrawl that is illegible to me. Emerging from his clothes, his limbs are etched with tattoos. Solidly. There's not one bare spot. Aaron's eyes light up when he talks about Jesus, and when he sings—with or without accompaniment—his head rolls back in worship. In a wilder moment, he contorts around the stage, hands gesturing with rhythmic and pointed accents to the music. The teens around him swirl, mosh, and head bang to the beat.

Just ask me to take Aaron's place and reach out to these kids myself. No. Don't. *I can't . . . I don't know how to relate to people who aren't like me.* I keep this pet excuse all sharpened and ready to pull out the instant I'm cornered by the unfamiliar. I don't speak Vietnamese. Homeless people smell. Safety says, "Don't talk to strangers." Especially manly men. My neighbors have large dogs, and I'm allergic. Whew. There. I'm off the hook now. I don't have to glow; I can go.

We're pretty much all-about-me people. No judgment here. It's just a fact. So when we consider sharing our faith with people outside our zone of comfort, it's natural that we clam up. *I can't . . . I don't know how to relate to people who aren't like me.* We lock in place. We can even take issue with those who look at life differently than we do, because if it's different, it's *wrong.* Rather than shining, our goal can slip into protecting.

Such a mode of being can be a mistake.

American Demographics reported that of the 4.1 million Americans who turned twenty-one in 2004,

25 percent were raised by a single parent;

61 percent favor legal gay marriage;

47 percent have a mobile phone;

93 percent have a credit card;

10 percent have credit card debt in excess of $7,000;

43 percent have a tattoo or body piercing;

41 percent currently live at home;

19 percent are married.

Do they sound like you? Or are they galaxies away from your world? Whether or not you and I "know them" or "are like them," they will be having babies, parenting, working, and living in our world as adults right alongside us for years to come. Will they notice the light of Jesus in us? Is our light in a container their culture can comprehend?

Josh is a philosophy student, pursuing his Ph.D. His head is covered in dreadlocks. His mind wraps around complex concepts like deconstructionism. His heart has journeyed toward, away from, and now back to Jesus. Josh is married to Lilly, a musician. Lilly has worked in a youth group abroad but now seeks meaning in her music and offers it as a pathway to others looking for hope. Josh and Lilly were raised in families that are very similar to my family. Today Josh and Lilly know God, the same God I know. I think. But they express their faith differently than I express mine. And the way they came to faith is very different from the way I came to faith.

Light is light. It doesn't change. But just as candles have given way to electricity in lighting our homes, our evangelistic light containers must also change to communicate with the culture of today. This view can be controversial, even creating a kind of Christian "star wars." Why? Probably because most of us like to find the "right" way to evangelize and then stick with it. In our day of ever-changing need, we can unwaveringly commit to the truth, but sticking with any one methodology for communicating truth may be unrealistic. This reality is uncomfortable and difficult to implement. Especially if we don't fully understand the culture around us today.

So let's do something about that. Let's understand—or at least try to understand—this world in which we live. Here's what I'm coming to grasp about lighting the way in our shifting culture.

Let's start with **postmodernism**. We live in a "postmodern" world. In days past (particularly the time period we call the "modern" age), everyone agreed on central values like objectivity, analysis, and control—all in the form of "blacks and whites" and "rights and wrongs." Today such absolutes are less compelling. Many postmodernists view the modern age when Western thought was intrinsically accepted as archaic. Who are they? While such individuals can be found in any age out there, most often they are in younger generations, and in the United States, more typically they inhabit urban settings in the north or on either coast.

Postmodern thinkers often view the way Christian "absolutes" are traditionally presented as putting a dark face on the offering of faith:

Arrogance—Christians expressing disdain and disrespect for other faiths as they emphasize that theirs is the "only true religion."

Judgmentalism—Christians evaluating others who believe differently or act differently as wrong, bad, and sinful.

Formula—Christians espousing a black-and-white formula for what it means to become a Christian and live the Christian life.

In an effort to respond to the rapidly growing presence of a postmodern worldview, many church leaders have designed worship services and outreach programs in "new containers" that can communicate the relevance of Jesus. This movement is labeled the **emerging church**. And some ingredients of such efforts include:

I can't . . . I don't know how to relate to people who aren't like me.

Authentic Community—Relationship is the key to ministry. People want to belong to a group for keeps, and in some circumstances this need takes priority over job commitments. There is a great desire for permanence. Interest in spiritual things as spiritual things is not hidden but straightforward.

Liturgical Practice—People want to attach to the origins of the Christian faith in a way that gives personal meaning. Mystery and wonder are important. There is a strong emphasis on the arts and all forms of liturgy.

Missional Attitude—Faith is to be lived out in action. Faith alone is not enough. The success of faith or of a church is evaluated through how many people go out into the world and serve as a result of what they are taught and believe.

Holistic Perspective—Faith impacts all aspects of life. Compartmentalization of being one person on Sunday and another person all week is disallowed.

Experiential Approach—People want to touch, feel, hear, see, and taste God in community, personally and all the time.

Doctrinal Diversity—There is less focus on denominations within Christianity and more respect for the basics of the faith across denominational lines.

Process Evangelism—Coming to Christ is a process. Questions around faith concern personal purpose and the meaning of life rather than the hereafter, heaven and hell, and "fire" insurance. Experience comes before explanation. Belonging comes before believing. Image comes before word.

Are we still in the Milky Way?

Here's where we're headed. Or rather, here's where we are. It's easy to flip into fear and reject whoever thinks differently from us as bad, wrong, or crazy. But the fact is that another manner of thinking may be none of these but just *different*. Rather than be freaked, frazzled, or fried, how about we shine? We live in a dark world. But God's light has come into us, and he calls us to twinkle.

I can't ... I don't know how to relate to people who aren't like me. The fact is that there are millions of people on our planet who are *unlike* us. In our discomfort with other worldviews, other cultures, other methods of thinking, we can grow defensive, judgmental, and exclusive. Rather than tiptoeing around cultural issues, Jesus cut through them. He spoke to a Samaritan woman in broad daylight (unheard of!), he told the religious leaders of the day just where they could stick their hard-to-get-into-heaven theology, and he made provision for *all* people—even Gentiles—to know God.

We need to move beyond a posture of fear, face the possible dangers of simple approaches, and make room for what God is doing in new ways of thinking. Nothing around us is a surprise to him.

Light is light. There's great comfort, security, and ... *power* in that. But penetrating the darkness of our day just may require our light *containers* to change.

That's why it's vital that we understand how our own generation and those generations around us approach the world. So that our containers can change to meet their worldview—without compromising our understanding of truth. This respect for cultural sensitivity isn't new to the twenty-first century. Paul displayed this attitude in 1 Corinthians 9:19, 22: "Though I am free and belong to no one, I have made myself a slave to everyone, to win as many as possible. . . . I have become all things to all people so that by all possible means I might save some."

Based on the research of experts like Robert Webber, Dan Kimball, Brian McLaren, Tim Keller, and others, let me suggest several helpful descriptors for each generation and how they react to spiritual truth and need. Be aware as you glance over these categories that individuals are individuals. You will encounter modern thinkers in the generations above you and postmodern thinkers in the generations below—and vice versa.

Generations Above:

Most often modern thinkers.

Communication is through words.

Belief is based on evidence or proof.

Church is a place for private worship. It is the religious voice for culture and the guide for moral behavior and is run by professional clergy.

Evangelism is accomplished by mass meetings with altar calls and with the use of tracts. Conversions are instant, through the sinner's prayer.

Generations Beside:

Combination of modern and postmodern thinkers.

Communication is instant and accomplished through technology.

Belief is based on "what works."

Church is a place to meet everyone's needs, to reach out to seekers and repair humanity, and is run by a business model.

Evangelism is accomplished by seeker services with an emphasis on a gradual conversion to a personal commitment to Christ.

Generations Below:

Most often postmodern thinkers.

Communication is interactive, through the Internet and community.

Belief comes through belonging.

Church is an incarnational community where people become Christ to a broken world. It functions as a countercultural community where the clergy and people partner to minister. Evangelism is a process whereby the church receives people who gradually come to faith through discipleship and mentorship and express their commitment in passage rites such as baptism.

Obviously there are some distinct differences from generation to generation. But remember: if we learn to understand how each generation approaches life and faith, we can learn to communicate with each effectively as we hold out truth and light to those around us.

Let's lay down our light sabers. There's no real need for star wars. Light is light. How we carry God's light to others and in what containers must change as our world changes. To a small Texas town's "Friday Night Lights" of football, we can be light. In New York City's 24-7 Times Square, we can be light. In a cabin in the woods of Wyoming surviving on a single kerosene flame, we can be light.

Twinkle—to the galaxies—and beyond!

"I have become all things to all people so that
by all possible means I might save some."
. . . .
1 Corinthians 9:22

FROM DARKNESS TO LIGHT

"Our conversion is not entirely our conversion. God is continually in the process of converting us—from our will to his way; from our fear to his assurance; from our efforts to his sufficiency; from our pursuit of the Christian life to an abandonment to his life within us."

Wayne Brown

I became a Christian when I was sixteen through the ministry of Young Life. At least I thought so until recently. Now I'm not so sure.

I grew up in a broken family. My parents were divorced when I was five years old. I saw my dad about once a year when he traveled out to the West Coast from his Florida home on business. My mom struggled with alcoholism. Along with my older sister and younger brother, I learned early on to fend for myself.

Central to my early memories are church, Jesus, and God. My mom would drop us off every Sunday for church and Sunday school and then pick us up a few hours later. Probably because we needed to fill hours at church, my sister and I joined the adult choir. I don't really know why they let us, but we sang every Sunday in our burgundy robes and creamy collar stoles. *Lo, how a rose e'er blooming . . .* I had no idea what most of the words meant, but I sang them from my heart.

From ever since I can remember, I have believed in God and loved him. Truly. Genuinely. Desperately. So you can imagine my dismay when much later in life (for me that meant sixteen), I was told that "becoming a Christian" meant praying a prayer to ask Jesus into my heart. Mercy! What had all the previous years been about? How could I have been so dense as to miss this step? Shame assaulted me. I felt that I'd been hanging out with Jesus as if he belonged to me when all along, I hadn't mouthed the required prayer to belong to him.

The heart issues of my parents' divorce and my assumed responsibility for their breakup lay under my easy absorption of shame. Peeling that away, I was left with the accusation that I'd done God "wrong" and needed to quickly and completely fix my mistake by doing him "right" and accepting him into my heart. Being the good girl, people-pleasing charmer that I was, I complied immediately. I prayed the prayer and became a Christian. Whew. There. Got it "right" this time.

Now I look back and see my grandiosity that I could "do God right" at all.

I became a Christian at sixteen, but now I know that my conversion began earlier. I just recently realized this. In my attempt to do God "right," I'd illegitimized the early stages of my journey, as if they didn't count because they didn't culminate in the appropriate final step: praying the sinner's prayer. Now I see that the early layers were the foundation for the culminating moment. If they hadn't been in place, would my choice have been clear?

I began to believe in Jesus in the neighborhood church on the West Coast where as a young child, I sang in the adult choir. When I was twelve years old, I was baptized. Sprinkled—as the Presbyterians do it. I was given a white children's Bible, and I carried it faithfully to and from church, fingering its rosy-edged pages and my name embossed on the cover in gold.

I continued to come to faith in Christ at thirteen while I walked down the upstairs Sunday school hall of another church in Houston, Texas. At the end was a display case holding portrait plates of Jesus and the disciples. As I approached the end of the hall and the mandatory right turn, I'd make eye contact with Jesus, and he wouldn't let me go. His eyes held mine. I knew he knew me. In late junior high school, I processed my options—bad kid crowd/good kid crowd—and sensed someone inside me steering me toward health. And my conversion continued.

When I was sixteen years old, I was ordained as an elder in the church—our congregation's response to the Jesus movement and their desire to include all generations in the Great Commission and leadership. I attended session meetings and helped serve communion.

Later on in my sixteenth year, I prayed the prayer to ask Jesus to come into my heart and "became a Christian."

If you're keeping tabs, that's sixteen years total just for me—one person—to become a Christian. (And that's counting the teeny tiny years before I even knew I was searching at age five.) *Sixteen years?* Yep. That's a long time. But some people take a lot longer.

Think here of light-years. A light-year is a unit of distance. It's the distance light travels in one year. Guess how far that is? Six trillion miles!!! So, when we say that something is traveling at the speed of light, that's fast. But it's also misleading. In the sky, the light of some of the stars we see tonight started out as far as six trillion miles away before making it to our atmosphere. The process of that light began a long, long, long way away. And we're just now seeing it. When we actually see a light from a star, we're seeing something that happened a very long time ago (sometimes in a galaxy far, far away).

God's work in the lives of those on the way to him began long before we came into a relationship with them. And it'll probably go on long after we're out of their lives. Evangelism isn't about a finite investment of time and energy. Rather, evangelism is a layered offering of light, over time, in various degrees of brilliance. Sometimes dim. Sometimes clear. Other times bright and clear.

I once heard an illustration that becoming a Christian can look different for different people. For some, it's as if they went to sleep in a room and left the window curtains open. At some point while they slept, light came into the dark room through the uncovered window. They couldn't say exactly when. All they know is that they went to bed in the dark and awoke in the light.

For others, becoming a Christian is a more definite experience, as if before they went to sleep, they drew the curtains shut. They awoke in a dark room, but when they went to the window and opened the curtains, light came into the room. They could look at their watch and note the exact moment.

In the first example, conversion seems to be about our gradual response to God's revelation of himself in our lives. In the second example, conversion is a specific moment in time when we recognize the very real presence of God. In both examples, salvation is clear and definite, though veiled in mystery.

In both examples, God waits until the nonbeliever "gets it" in his or her own time and his or her own circumstances. How that happens is personal. How that happens is a process. For those of us involved in helping an unbeliever along the way, that process can be painfully slow or amazingly quick.

I thought I became a Christian when I was sixteen. But I'd been becoming a Christian for a long time before that. And while I know my salvation is absolutely secure today, I am still very much becoming who God wants me to be even as I write.

There is a process to conversion, short for some people, longer for others. An example of short? The Gospels give many examples of those who were healed and *immediately* follow Jesus. In John 4, Jesus meets a woman at a well, asks her a few penetrating questions, and in the amount of time it takes to draw a jug, she chooses him and the living water he offers. The centurion described in Matthew 8 needed but a few moments to have faith in Jesus. In all such cases, the change, the result, the *acknowledgment* of faith is quick and clear.

The Bible also gives examples of other, more lengthy conversions. In John 3, Nicodemus came to Jesus in the night to find out more about God. Just when Nicodemus "accepted" truth into his heart we aren't told specifically, but later as he accompanies the body of Jesus with Joseph in John 19:39, we know that he is on the believing rather than the doubting side.

Jesus' words to Nicodemus guide each of us as we convert—or turn from unbelief to belief, from death to life, and from darkness to light.

> For God so loved the world that he gave his one and only Son, that whoever believes in him shall not perish but have eternal life. For God did not send his Son into the world to condemn the world, but to save the world through him. Whoever believes in him is not condemned, but whoever does not believe stands condemned already because they have not believed in the name of God's one and only Son. This is the verdict: Light has come into the world, but people loved darkness instead of light because their deeds were evil. All those who do evil hate the light, and will not come into the light for fear that their deeds will be exposed. But those who live by the truth come into the light, so that it may be seen plainly that what they have done has been done in the sight of God.
>
> *John 3:16–21*

Just as there is a process to conversion, evangelism is a process. Gradually, God layers the light until the one in darkness recognizes it and responds and salvation occurs.

Evangelism is a process. In the end, the *I can'ts* and the *I cans* aren't really the issue. The issue is light and whether or not it is present in the darkness. We can move past the *I can'ts* to the *I cans* by understanding that our light is part of a galaxy of lights—some seen with immediate results and some more gradually taking place.

We need to shine, and shine, and continue to shine. All of us. In all of our containers. To all the world. While we don't have control over when and how the one in darkness will respond—that is truly the work of the Holy Spirit—we do have the choice to be bright lights to light the way of hope for others. In time, the results will be revealed.

"For God so loved the world that he gave his one and only Son, that whoever believes in him shall not perish but have eternal life.... But those who live by the truth come into the light, so that it may be seen plainly that what they have done has been done in the sight of God."
....
John 3:16, 21

PART TWO

Grabbing On to the *I Cans*

A young boy walked along the beach one evening. He came upon a starfish, stranded yards from the tide, struggling for life. The boy reached down and gently lifted the starfish and returned it to the ocean.

A man approached the boy and asked, "Why are you bothering with that starfish? They die up tide all the time, by the hundreds. That won't make a difference."

Raising his eyes to the man, the young boy said, "It'll make a difference to this one."

Source Unknown

I can . . . **accept others the way they are.**

be a friend.

be real.

help my children know the Jesus I know.

offer hope in the daily minutes of life.

partner with others.

offer help and hope in crisis.

serve.

accept the doubts in others.

share my faith at holidays.

leave room for wonder.

keep trying even when it seems
hopeless.

trust God with the results of my efforts.

leave a legacy of light.

"Some wish to live
within the sound
of a church or chapel bell;
I want to run a rescue shop
within a yard of Hell."

C. T. Studd

Relaxed in my poolside chair, I flipped the pages of a magazine. It was one of those rarest of rare Sunday afternoons when I'd said I'd take the kids to the pool, they actually wanted to go, and the weather was perfect. Past the age of requiring my help to adjust goggles and water wings, my kids were in eyesight across the pool playing with friends. I was enjoying five minutes of peace.

My attention was suddenly diverted to an audibly upset man a few feet away. Dragging his toddler from the pool, he hurled angry words at a group of teenagers. "Can't you watch your language? That kind of talk has no place in front of children!"

His eyes met mine, even through our sunglasses. "Have they been talking like that very long?" he asked.

Embarrassed, I responded, "You know, I really hadn't noticed. . . . I was reading."

At that moment, my then ten-year-old daughter, Eva, approached, having taken in the scene herself. Eight-year-old Ethan wasn't far behind. As we gathered our gear to go home, Eva asked me why the man had been so upset. I told them some teenagers had been swearing, and he was concerned about his toddler overhearing. "What did they say?" she asked.

"I don't really know—I was reading. But I think the 's' word and the 'f' word." I thought this over and asked Eva, "Do you ever hear that kind of language at school or in the neighborhood?"

She didn't even hesitate in her response. "Sure. All the time." Though at this point in my parenting life I was still on the naive side, I realized this was probably to be expected.

"What do you think when you hear people talk like that?"

Her response was again immediate. "I guess I figure they don't know God and don't know that he wouldn't want them to talk that way."

In 1 Corinthians 2:14 and 16, Paul writes a very similar statement: "The person without the Spirit does not accept the things that come from the Spirit of God but considers them foolishness, and cannot understand them because they are discerned only through the Spirit. . . . But we have the mind of Christ." I don't know whether the father at the pool was incensed because the swearing offended him for spiritual reasons or because he was a man disappointed by the immorality of the world in which his son would grow. I do know that Eva's response made sense to me then and makes sense to me now as I hold out my little light to the dark places in my world. When it comes to sharing my faith with others, *I can accept people the way they are.*

This isn't a world that knows and loves God. We shouldn't expect it to be. People who don't yet know God won't act like they do. As someone put it, we need to understand that they just don't understand. So when we go to shine—we need to forgo expectations as to how people in the dark will be acting in the presence of God's light. We need to let go of the no-no's.

It's Bunco night in the neighborhood. To go or not to go? No doubt, God wants to shine his light in the darkness. There are folks in darkness at the Bunco party. You've got God's light in you. But there will be drinking and smoking and foul language and lousy moral standards.

Right. Sometimes folks who don't know God act like that. (Sometimes those who do know God act like that too.)

Take it up a notch. You're thinking of hosting a holiday gathering in your home. You've been getting to know a few co-workers and feel it's time to get more personal. Yet you hesitate. One man is gay. He might want to bring a date. A guy date. Maybe you could tell him it's for family only. But would you say that to a woman who wanted to bring her boyfriend? What if that same woman's boyfriend was a live-in boyfriend?

Evangelism can get so complicated. A simple open house becomes a moral dilemma. Such issues can wrap themselves around our light until they threaten to snuff it out. They can create a "bushel" and hide our light from the darkest spots so desperately in need of illumination.

Here's the reality: Jesus doesn't ask people to change their lifestyles and behavior before coming to him. Why should we? Jesus accepts people exactly as they are, habits, foibles, and all. Transformation from one kind of life to another occurs *after* people know Jesus and as they respond to his love in their lives. If Jesus doesn't require someone to clean up before believing, why should we?

Take a minute to list the no-no's you tend to impose on others. Include items like behavior, thought, wardrobe, language, and associations . . . oh, and another biggie: political position. Now take a good look at your list. Does Jesus take a stance on these issues? For or against? While there are some obvious standards for behavior as a follower of Christ, where have you seen him mandate conformance to those standards as a prerequisite to *coming to* faith?

One more step. How can you take your list of no-no's and turn it into icebreakers for getting a conversation started? I'm constantly amazed at how the very item I tend to judge or evaluate in another's life can become the springboard to connection.

Like the time I saw a mom just about haul off and slap her three-year-old in the grocery store aisle. She almost lost it—totally. At that moment I happened to wheel my cart down the aisle, she glanced up, and simply due to the presence of another human, she gathered up her emotions and composed herself.

I wanted to U-turn it and leave. She spelled trouble. Maybe it was because I'd often been so close to such a complete meltdown myself as a young mom, but I didn't run. I met her eyes and offered a very sincere, "Life is really hard" shrug. She sighed, lifted her chin a bit, and continued.

It was a very small gesture, a twinkle of light, but I believe it offered her a ray of hope in a dark moment.

BUT! If we overlook the blunders of others, won't we grow "soft" toward our own spiritual development, excusing the very actions and attitudes that Jesus longs to change? Hey. Here's the truth: not one of us is without error, and not one of us is removed from temptation. Accepting the imperfections in others doesn't mean we ignore them in ourselves. We need to ask ourselves how *we're* growing, how *we're* handling our weak spots. Sometimes we can worry so much about where everybody else is messing up that we forget to grow ourselves.

Okay. Now back to the no-no's we see in others.

Jesus went to dinner with sinners. He hung out with prostitutes and gamblers. He touched those who were diseased and equally offered himself to those on the right and left of the political issues of his day. Jesus knows the hearts of those created by God and loves them. We can do the same. Our lives will shine more brightly in the darkest spots if we let go of the no-no's that cover our beams. *I can accept people the way they are* and leave it to Jesus to do the "redecorating" of their behavior.

"But we have the mind of Christ."
....
1 Corinthians 2:16

accept others the way they are.

I can . . . **be a friend.**

be real.

help my children know the Jesus I know.

offer hope in the daily minutes of life.

partner with others.

offer help and hope in crisis.

serve.

accept the doubts in others.

share my faith at holidays.

leave room for wonder.

keep trying even when it seems
    hopeless.

trust God with the results of my efforts.

leave a legacy of light.

"You are a Christian today
because somebody cared.
Now it's
your turn."

Warren Wiersbe

The state of Texas is very proud of its nickname: The Lone Star State. The nickname comes from the single gold star embedded in a night-sky blue background. The lone star symbolizes Texas as an independent republic and serves as a reminder of the state's fight for independence from Mexico. Contrasting to this statement of independence, the state motto for Texas is "Friendship," as the word "Texas" originates from the word *teysha* meaning "hello friend" in the native language of the Caddo Indian tribes. I know this because after my initial California days, I spent the rest of my growing up in Texas. (And because I looked this up on the Internet.) Texans will take you in their arms and squeeze you till you have no air left in your chest. 'Course the humidity there will suck the life out of your lungs as well.

I remember my mom's friends in Texas, leftovers from her college sorority days. They called themselves "The Ranch Gang," and true to their label, they hung out every summer on the front porch of one member's ranch, swapping stories, recipes, laughter, and tears. These were Texas gals. They gathered each other together and held on tight. They *belonged* to each other.

When it comes to its people, Texas' nickname is overshadowed by its motto. Independence gives way to friendship.

Belonging is a powerful experience. When we check our independence at the door and plop down in the company of a friend, we've opened ourselves to involvement, investment, and possibly, to intimacy.

When we belong to something, that thing changes us. We belong to a club—we're known as *members*. We belong to a clique—we're *in*. We belong to a spouse through marriage—we're *husband and wife*. We belong to a child through birth or adoption—we're *parents*. Yep. Belonging changes us big time.

But not as much as believing changes us. Believing changes us even more than belonging. Believing makes us think and choose and invest *because we belong*. In the spiritual realm, belonging usually precedes believing. People want relationships with us before they'll consider a relationship with God. So when it comes to twinkling, there's a very important *I can* to consider: *I can be a friend.*

Where I work, at MOPS International, friendship as a means of evangelism is core. Jamie tells of a woman who wanted to be friends with her before being friends with God:

> Last year a mom called and was very pointed in asking me about "how spiritual" our group was. She made it very clear that she might be interested in attending a meeting but she didn't want anything to do with church or religion or anything spiritual. At her first MOPS meeting, she sat with her arms crossed the whole time. Gradually she has opened up. She even started coming to church, attending spiritually oriented women's events! Now she helps with the children for the morning group and comes to the evening group. She is much more open to spiritual conversations. I try to keep this in mind as people call about coming to MOPS for the first time. We never know what seeds are being planted if we are open to opportunities.

Belonging comes before believing. People come into friendship with us as a kind of trial run for a possible friendship with the God we love. Will we take the risk and befriend these "lone stars"?

I met Argelia when I worked in a file room for a medical practice. I was seventeen. She was in her fifties. I spoke English. She spoke Spanish. She was a grandmother. I wasn't even married. Initially our conversations consisted of how the alphabet had been color coded for filing ease and how much time to take during a break. Later, over tuna sandwiches and Diet Cokes at the picnic table outside our building, we swapped stories of growing up, parents, guys (to her they were men), and eventually, faith. Argelia was Catholic. We spent many lunch hours comparing the experience of the Catholic Church with that of the Presbyterian. Why did she have to go "through the priest" to confess her sins to Jesus? How could I pray straight to Jesus? Who was Mary to her and to me?

But before we got to sharing our beliefs at this level, we belonged to each other in friendship. That's just the order in which it works.

The thing about belonging is that it doesn't work one way. The kind of belonging that leads to believing has to be mutual, two-way belonging.

Sandi has been doing my nails for about six years. I met her in a shop near my home. I'd delayed the nail thing as long as possible. I was busy with mothering and ministry. But one day I saw a photo of myself and reconsidered. There I was: reasonably pulled-together outfit, hip hair, decent makeup. And my stubby fingers wrapped around a soda can. Ugly nails. It was time. So I sought out a shop nearby. The receptionist booked me with Sandi.

Our first meeting was warm as we exchanged surface details: I had two kids. She had two. Mine were a decade or so ahead of hers. I was married. She was married. My husband worked out of our house in Christian distance education. Hers was in construction.

My second appointment was uncomfortable. Novice that I was, I figured that if I was paying to have nails applied, I was paying every week for a full set. So at the end of my second week, just before my second appointment, I chewed them off. All of them.

I sat down opposite Sandi, planning to pick up where we'd left off at the prior appointment. But as she took my hands in hers, a silent fury overtook her. It was palpable. She worked without a word, gluing and filling and filing an entire new set of nails for my stubs. I couldn't figure out what I'd done wrong until her next appointment arrived—and sat waiting another half hour for Sandi to finish me. Finally, Sandi sighed and bellowed over my shoulder at an increasingly impatient client, "Sorry I'm so late—I had to put a whole new set of nails on her—since last week!"

Duh. Rebase. I learned the concept the hard way. I was embarrassed of course. But looking back, my "need" for Sandi invited her need for me. There was a mutuality at work here. A friendship. Would we have forged this open friendship—where no topic is barred—if I hadn't been revealed as such a loser in our second week? I wonder.

We've talked about child rearing, marriage, work, dogs, vacations, sex, and housecleaning. When she approached her thirtieth birthday, she teared up and talked about her life's purpose. When my teenagers bumped along in unsuccessful seasons of struggle, I confessed them to her, along with my hope that Jesus would eventually see them through.

Most of the time I didn't know what to say to Sandi about Jesus. I just loved her in the daily and let her love me back. Sure, I invited her to church, took her to hear me speak, talked with her about God, and prayed for her. But beneath these gestures, I felt unsteady and unsure and uncertain that my light twinkled. Today Sandi has moved from wondering about the difference Jesus might make in her life to wondering how people who don't know him get through the day. I don't really know how it all happened. But I really think it was the belonging thing that worked over finally into believing.

In 1 Thessalonians 2:8, Paul underlines this very human quality of linking belonging and belief. "We loved you so much that we were delighted to share with you not only the gospel of God but our lives as well, because you had become so dear to us."

Belonging involves sharing all of life—mutually. Pushing past the temptation to stall in independence, belonging chooses friendship and allows friendship to affect belief. Belonging changes us. It changes who we are and what we believe. *I can be a friend.*

The stars shine bright . . . deep in the heart of Texas! And everywhere we choose to twinkle.

"We were delighted to share with you not only the gospel of God

but our lives as well."
. . . .
1 Thessalonians 2:8

I can . . .

accept others the way they are.

be a friend.

be real.

help my children know the Jesus I know.

offer hope in the daily minutes of life.

partner with others.

offer help and hope in crisis.

serve.

accept the doubts in others.

share my faith at holidays.

leave room for wonder.

keep trying even when it seems
  hopeless.

trust God with the results of my efforts.

leave a legacy of light.

"Lord, make me like crystal that your light may shine through me."

Katherine Mansfield

Think for a minute. What person has had the greatest impact on your life? No fair picking a celebrity. Pick a regular person. Someone you know up close and personal. Now—think again, why were you so impressed with this person? Was it because they modeled maturity—perfectly? Because they conquered areas where you are challenged?

I have a hunch that we're most impacted not by perfection but by reality.

When I was newly married, I glued my eyes on a couple who lived close by. Because I came from a divorced family, my concept of marriage was, well, clueless. Watching Bob and Linda mapped out marriage for me. They laughed. They divvied up household responsibilities. They hugged and kissed and more. They argued. They didn't hide their growing pains or their victories, and in the process of being vulnerable, they made marriage believable.

When it comes to sharing our faith, I'm convinced that living up close and personal is essential to the process of introducing others to Christ. Who wants to follow after a fake? Vulnerability is believability, and faith becomes believable when it's lived out by vulnerable followers of Christ. *I can be real.*

In its simplest form, vulnerability—being real—means to be open to hurt. It embraces the reality of risk. Jesus modeled vulnerability edgily, honestly, and consistently. When he visited his hometown of Nazareth, he didn't try to wow people with his God-ness. He simply spoke the truth. He didn't pretend it didn't hurt to be rejected by his Father when hanging on the cross for our sins. While Jesus never sinned, he struggled with temptation just as any human. By being vulnerable, God made himself believable.

Our relationship with Jesus sets us apart from living just any old way according to any old value system, but it doesn't set us apart from speaking into human life. It's funny how in certain settings, the topic of my faith pops up, and a veil falls down over the conversation. In some situations, I see fear running across faces, and I can almost hear minds clicking back over previous conversations for "mistakes." A barrier locks in place between me and those around me who don't yet know God, and I find myself either hoisted up to a plane of perfection that religious people occupy or relegated to a remote planet where weird "believers" exist.

Here I face some choices. I can safely sit up in my world of togetherness, tucking my struggles with sin out of sight. Yes, Jesus makes all things new—fabulous! Or, wincing at the perceived rejection, I can turn tail and run. I share in the sufferings of Christ!

Or I can risk. *I can be real.*

What's it going to be? Well, what twinkles the most? Where is more light more clearly seen?

Our family has been through lots. Lots of challenges. Lots of joys. Lots of predictable and lots of unpredictable messes. My husband survived cancer. We've both seen our parents die. My children have made choices that make my heart twist. You know what I've discovered as I've navigated through these life surgeries? People are watching. People who know Jesus *and* people still on the way to him. While no one *applauds* the issues I've faced, everyone seems to turn to see what I'll do with what I've got.

"Oh! Here's a woman who knows God and doesn't have it all together! Wow! Maybe I can figure out from her how to make my life work too!" They watch not for how perfectly I maneuver but for how I put one foot in front of the other and shuffle along. I think this open-book living is what got Sandi and me over the bumpiness in our early friendship.

Punch the pause button for a minute now. I haven't always responded so openly, with vulnerability, to the watching eyes around me. I haven't always been willing to be real. In earlier years, most of my efforts were aimed at looking good on the outside, no matter what was going on inside. I'd swallowed the lie that if you know God, life is good. Bad stuff won't happen. So when bad stuff did happen, I'd feel like it was my fault and like I had to protect God's reputation so that he'd look good in spite of the mess of me.

One day an acquaintance confronted me. "Elisa, why can't you ever be real? You always seem so perfect! Why can't you get down off your pedestal and be messed up like the rest of us?"

After that incident I did some painful self-examination. What I found is that her blunt and hard-to-hear words were accurate. I began to see that I really wasn't very real about who I was. I was willing to share about past lessons I'd learned but not about the everyday continuing issues I hid within. I thought I was supposed to be perfect, when the fact is that I'm not and God is allowing me to be stretched today so that someday I'll look more like him. ("A life unexamined is a life not worth living." Thank you, Socrates!)

Others need to see his work in progress that is me.

Being real means modeling the *process* of Christianity, not just the *product.* When we model only the product, only the end result of what Jesus can do, we give only half the story and confuse those who watch. We show our great strides in spirituality, and people become frustrated in response. They know what they're supposed to look like, but they don't know how to get there.

But when we choose as our goal to model the process of faith, we demonstrate through words, actions, and attitudes that we're in the process of becoming like Jesus. By modeling the process, we encourage onlookers to jump on board and go with us. Rather than puffing behind someone they can never catch, they learn alongside, seeing *how* to yield, *how* to relinquish, *how* to get up from a fall and begin again. Further, modeling the process and not the product reveals God's work in us, mincing into tiny pieces the temptation to take the credit for the work ourselves.

In 2 Corinthians 4:7, Paul characterizes the people of God as clay jars holding the treasures of God's gospel. Carrying forward the New Testament custom of keeping treasures in earthen pots, he writes, "But we have this treasure in jars of clay to show that this all-surpassing power is from God and not from us."

Isn't that what we want others to know? That the power is from God and not from us? That the light we shine has God as its source? That because the light that's shining isn't from us or about us, others too can have this hope in their days?

God calls us to be see-through stars, lights that transparently communicate the ongoing nature of how we are changed by him through being related to him. *I can be real.*

Vulnerability means living a resurrected life with the scars of nail prints still visible in your hands.

"But we have this treasure in jars of clay to show that this all-surpassing power is

from God and not from us."
....
2 Corinthians 4:7

accept others the way they are.

be a friend.

be real.

I can . . . **help my children know the Jesus I know.**

offer hope in the daily minutes of life.

partner with others.

offer help and hope in crisis.

serve.

accept the doubts in others.

share my faith at holidays.

leave room for wonder.

keep trying even when it seems hopeless.

trust God with the results of my efforts.

leave a legacy of light.

"The little child,
when it sees a star sparkle,
stretches out its dimpled arm.
It wants that star.
To want a star is the beautiful
insanity of the young."

Countess de Gasparin

I t had been a busy morning. The cleaners. Then the library. Haircuts. Finally the grocery store. My son, Ethan (then in the early elementary years), and I pulled into the garage and began the process of carrying in our loads from the car. Mine: bags of groceries. Ethan's: armloads of toys. We'd both learned well the lesson that errands go better if Ethan is occupied. And so on errand days, he armed himself with piles of entertainment for the "just in case I get bored" moments.

"Mom! My binoculars! They're not here!" a voice of alarm leapfrogged over the half-wall separating family room and kitchen.

Yikes. We'd been to a gazillion places. In and out of the car. To and from stores. Perhaps he'd mislaid them here at home and hadn't taken them along. Ethan seemed positive he'd put them in his backpack and had played with them at some errand stop, but just to be sure, we split up and scoured the house. I looked under beds and couches and in closets. He inspected his room. We met on the stair landing, empty-handed. I couldn't think of anywhere else to look, and taking in his furrowed face, I was worried. "Ethan, I don't know where else to look! I think they're lost, honey." I reached down, offering comfort.

Keenly, Ethan studied my face. "Mom, we may not know where they are, but Jesus does. Why don't we just ask him?" he asked.

Amazing. As a mom, I had spent many days, months, and years noodling over how I could make God real to my children. Most of the time I felt like a flop in this mothering category. Suddenly, here was Ethan, empty-handed from his thorough search for his beloved binoculars, fully convinced that Jesus knew what he did not and therefore that Jesus could find what he could not.

Ethan had a point: Jesus knew. He'd been with us all morning long. He was in our entrances and our exits. He went with us to and from the car. He knew our ways. He knew our "going out and our lying down." Of course, he knew where the binoculars were. He could see them even now.

On the stair landing in our home, I followed my son's lead and bowed my head. We acknowledged that Jesus knew where Ethan's binoculars were. We asked him to show us. Then we climbed back into our seat belts, backed out of the garage, and retraced our steps through our morning errands. Back to the cleaners. The library. At the hair place, the receptionist welcomed us warmly, holding up a pair of very familiar binoculars. "Are you here for these?" she questioned. "I found them under a chair and remembered Ethan playing with them. I figured you'd be back!"

Ethan embraced his binoculars and winked up at me. "Well, we didn't know *exactly* where they were, but we knew Someone else did and that he'd show us!"

Sounds too good to be true, doesn't it? A child's simple faith. And yet this moment has held me tightly to another *I can* in sharing my faith. *I can help my children know the Jesus I know.*

Most of us bow under the weight of more than a few questions about children and how they come to faith. How do children believe? When are they able to believe?

Clearly, belief is possible for children. Jesus said in Luke 18:16, "Let the little children come to me, and do not hinder them, for the kingdom of God belongs to such as these." Like Ethan in his binocular search, somehow, kids get Jesus. They recognize light and are drawn to it.

My children are now adults. Young adults, but they are adults. While raised in the same home by the same parents with basically the same spiritual teaching (Jesus time just about every night, Bible songs, plenty of talk about Jesus), their journeys toward God have differed from each other's, and from their father's and from mine.

Eva and Ethan asked Jesus to come into their hearts when they were five and three years old, respectively. It was near Christmas. I'd done a teaching in children's church on the "gift of Jesus," and when we got home, Evan and I talked with them separately about whether or not they wanted to accept this gift. While we hesitated to "manipulate" them into the kingdom, we also didn't want to miss a moment of readiness. Were they ready? Each was. Each bowed and prayed with us.

Through the years that followed, we continued having Jesus time, praying together, and learning about God in Sunday school and in everyday life. As my children matured, youth group was big for them both. There they made friends, watched their youth leaders role model the faith, and participated in missions trips abroad to impoverished worlds.

In their teen years, both my children questioned God. For a season, Eva bolted from the lifestyle in which she'd been raised, but even in her time away, she now reports that she felt God's presence. Upon her return, she eventually recommitted her life to God and pursues a relationship with Jesus today.

Ethan held on to God a bit longer but began to question his faith on a more philosophical ground. He's still traveling toward truth, investigating, wondering, and at times, denying a need for God.

When my children have hit such bumps along their spiritual treks, I've questioned: just what was it that happened in their early years? Was their commitment to Christ real? Did they mean it? Did they understand it? I think back to moments like Ethan's binocular search, or his buck-naked from-the-shower six-year-old pronouncement, "Jesus Christ is the Son of God who died on the cross for our sins!" or Eva's wide-eyed comprehension at age five that the disciples had left everything to follow Jesus, and a certainty rises up inside me.

Like all of us, children come to Jesus in a process. Whether at three or five or twelve or sixteen or twenty-one years of age, like us, children can give all they know of themselves to all they know of Jesus. And like us, the process of coming to Christ continues as the process of human development continues. The more we discover, the more we have to surrender. Tiny twinkles grow into true lights.

As moms and dads and teachers and pastors and shapers of children, our job is to influence them. God's job is to reveal himself to them. Their job is to seek faith for themselves. How can we do our part? Here are some "little light" suggestions to layer into the days of your young:

Create a regular "Jesus time." For us it was after dinner or before bed. We used devotional books, children's Bibles, music, and finger games. Providing a simple, predictable time to talk about God is vital to young ones. They grow to expect discussion. Questions bubble up in their minds. Prayer becomes a habit.

Give each child a Bible. There's something very special—and sacred— about sharing the privilege of Bible carrying and reading and holding with the very young. Graduate each reading level with that of your child. My daughter adored her Teen Study Bible beyond her teen years, largely due to the familiar "feel" and gobs of pictures, notes, and bookmarks stuck in its pages.

Find a church family. Miss Debbie taught our children throughout the elementary years. They looked forward to her warm hug and happy face each Sunday. Beyond those years, youth group leaders invested in their lives and made the difference in whether or not they'd drag themselves out of bed and into their own cars and drive the distance to church.

Keep a journal for perspective. As adults, there are times when we can see what God is doing in our children's lives, and remember it better than they can. Because I chronicled Ethan's binocular story years ago, I can tell it to him today. Would we otherwise have it to help along the way?

Sign up for service together. When children see the needs of others, they grow in their understanding of how Jesus meets their own needs. Whether Prison Fellowship's Angel Tree program at Christmas, or Compassion International's Sponsor a Child, allowing a child to help another person leaves a lasting impact. After his involvement in an Operation Christmas Child's shoe box distribution, Ethan swore off his customary Christmas greed. "I don't need new shoes, Mom. These kids don't even have shoes," he lamented.

Build meaning into the holidays and holy days. I fully enjoy the secular celebrations attached to many of our holy days. They're fun. But without the meaning underlying such memorials, the days and nights are throwaway fun. Take the time to underline God's gift of his Son, Jesus, with a Jesus birthday celebration and a manger display at Christmas. Explain that Santa is a celebration begun by a Christian believer (named Nicholas) that commemorates the gifts brought by the Magi to Jesus. Pull apart the Easter Bunny and springtime rituals as distinct—and mythical—compared to the resurrection of Jesus from the dead and the new life he brings.

Children often begin their faith experience as tiny twinkles with sincere commitments to Jesus. As influencers, we can light the way home for them. *I can help my children know the Jesus I know.* As they grow, their faith must grow in the process of giving more of what they know about themselves to more of what they know about Jesus.

Every Christmas, I set out a nativity scene somewhere in our house. Locations have moved from mantel to piano top to foyer table. Characters have changed from burlap to gold filigreed over the years, depending on my mood and the decor of our celebration. But it's always there. In some seasons, my children have joined me in placing the characters "just so" around the baby Jesus. In others, I've arranged them to my own liking, painfully aware of my children's absence or disinterest.

Atop the manger is a star. Unchanging. Directing. Bright. Clear. Lighting the way home. I've often said, "If you ever lose your way, just follow the star. It lights the pathway home."

Back on the day when Ethan lost his binoculars, he was completely convinced that Jesus knew where they were. Today, as my children journey toward God, I lean on the truth that Jesus knows where my daughter and my son are. They are within his sight . . . tiny twinkles on their way home.

"Let the little children come to me, and do not hinder them,

for the kingdom of God belongs to such as these."
. . . .
Luke 18:16

accept others the way they are.

be a friend.

be real.

help my children know the Jesus I know.

I can . . . **offer hope in the daily minutes
of life.**

partner with others.

offer help and hope in crisis.

serve.

accept the doubts in others.

share my faith at holidays.

leave room for wonder.

keep trying even when it seems
hopeless.

trust God with the results of my efforts.

leave a legacy of light.

"We have this moment,
sparkling like a
    star
    in
    our
    hand . . .
and
    melting
        like a snowflake."

Lisa King

W hy do you wear that cross around your neck?" The question came from Bryan, a kindergarten buddy of my then-six-year-old, Ethan. As Ethan tells it, he looked at Bryan and replied, "Because I'm a Christian. And Jesus died on a cross and was raised from the dead."

So far, so good, I thought, as Ethan relayed the conversation over the dinner table. "What did Bryan say then?" I asked.

"He said that stuff about Jesus wasn't true. I told him it was *so* true."

It went on like this for a while, between bites of spaghetti and swallows of milk, the description of Bryan's questions and Ethan's defense of his faith. A tiny twinkle before a tiny darkness.

Life is filled with moments like this. Shooting stars that whiz through our days, easy to miss. Like Bryan. He was just a kid, my son's playground buddy. He wasn't around for more than a school semester or so, but he came into Ethan's life and therefore into the life of our family for a season, and the light of our lives touched his life a bit. I have no idea if he noticed. But he came. And he questioned. So we twinkled in response because this is what we can do: twinkle. *I can offer hope in the daily minutes of my life.*

Then there's the interaction I had with Mike, my cleaners guy. Meeting his gaze over an armload of drycleaning, I found Mike's normally bright eyes cloudy with concern. "What's up, Mike?" I asked as I laid down my load.

"The tsunami. What do you think of that, Mrs. Morgan? It's freaking me out!"

As I sorted out dry cleanable items from laundry ones, I pondered my response. I'd often wondered about Mike's spiritual orientation. His heritage was Asian, from where specifically or how many generations in the States, I didn't know. Every time I entered his store, good weather or bad, early in the day or late, whether crowded or empty, his attitude was nothing less than *precious*. When he handed me back my credit card, he did so with both hands—and a little bow. His whole being emanated joy, but its source was unclear to me.

I chose the widest response I could think of to Mike's question: another question. "Well, Mike, what do *you* think of the tsunami? Why are you freaked out?"

"Well, I think these days are like the end days the Bible describes!"

Now he had me. Or I had him, depending on how you looked at it. "Tell me more about what you're thinking, Mike."

He responded, "You know, like the book of Revelation!" His eyebrows punctuated this last book of the Bible with their own authoritative period.

"Mike . . . are you a Christian?" There are very few moments when I get this direct, but this was one of them.

"You bet, Mrs. Morgan," came his eager reply.

"I am too, Mike. And I guess what I think of the tsunami is that if we know Jesus, then he expects us to trust him during this tragedy and any other mess up ahead. If we know God, then we know that he's in charge of our days."

Mike smiled, sighed, and handed me my credit card receipt—with a little bow. "That's right, Mrs. Morgan. That's what I know I would hear in church. I just guess I needed to be reminded." Don't we all?

I exited the cleaners that day reminded that it is in the "everyday" minutes of life that twinkling is so important. Both before those who know God and before those still on the way.

People come in and out of our lives—through family members, through workplace connections, through impromptu meetings in the park. In such moments we become like shooting stars—whistling through their lives with a streak of light. What was *that*? Most of the time, we don't think much of such interactions. As with little Bryan a decade ago, we have no idea if the light of our lives is impacting the darkness in theirs or not. In rare moments we find out years later. *You were the one who first connected me with God—remember the time . . . ?* But most of the time, someone bumps our shoulder in the checkout line, sits by us on an airplane, parents the child our child befriends, signs up to lead the Girl Scout troop the same year we sign up . . . and we never really know whether our twinkling changed their darkness or not.

It's so easy to overlook the value of twinkling in seemingly insignificant spots. We're tempted to rate as worthy of the effort only the really big moments in life—the crises, the immediate family relationship, the boyfriend we wish we could marry but who doesn't yet share our faith—or the people we personally pick to be in our days.

It's also easy to overlook the value of uncensored twinkling. This means "letting our light shine" in our conversations and our interactions and not cutting God out of what we communicate. Sure, it's wise to avoid the "Christianese" sharing that nonbelievers simply can't comprehend, but we don't have to *hide* our faith either. Let it shine!

In 2 Timothy 4:2, we're encouraged to "preach the Word; be prepared in season and out of season; correct, rebuke and encourage—with great patience and careful instruction." These are strong words. Not all of us are comfortable with the concept of "preaching the Word" 24/7. Comfort returns when we realize that Paul is encouraging Timothy and us to be ready to *speak the needed word whenever* the situation requires. That means twinkle in the small moments and the large, in the obvious spots and in the hidden ones, with people we choose and with people chosen for us. We can do this—if we choose to.

While I'm on the subject of being a shooting star, let me take another angle. Yes, we can twinkle in small spots, gently sharing our light in another's darkness—and that twinkling can make a huge difference. But we can also twinkle like a shooting star more directly, asking the direct questions and insisting on black and white answers.

I'd been teaching a neighborhood Bible study for about a year when Rebecca, a friend who lived a subdivision over from us, approached me with some very specific questions. They started with, "Where should I start reading in the Bible? I've never read it before." Months later our conversation culminated with a zinger of a question: "What do you think I ought to do next? I don't think I have the Jesus you're talking about in my life."

So we sat down in my living room. I explained that she could ask Jesus to be in her life permanently by admitting her need for him and inviting him to lead her life and be in charge. She eagerly agreed. We bowed our heads and prayed.

I kind of always thought someone else would pray that way with Rebecca. I assumed that I was just the one to teach the Bible. Somebody else would close the deal. But in a moment it became clear that I was to shine in that spot—a spot that might not return again in such clarity. Like Bryan with Ethan. Like Mike at the cleaners.

I can offer hope in my daily minutes of life. Sometimes the hope I offer is a subtle twinkle. In other moments, my shooting star is direct, aimed like an arrow at the bull's-eye of conversion.

"Be prepared in season and out of season."
. . . .
2 Timothy 4:2

I can . . .

accept others the way they are.

be a friend.

be real.

help my children know the Jesus I know.

offer hope in the daily minutes of life.

partner with others.

offer help and hope in crisis.

serve.

accept the doubts in others.

share my faith at holidays.

leave room for wonder.

keep trying even when it seems
  hopeless.

trust God with the results of my efforts.

leave a legacy of light.

"As a single star,
our sun is in a minority:
more than half the stars
in the sky have at least
one companion in space."

David H. Levy

Ever feel a little lonely in the lighting business? Do something about it. Partner with another. We don't have to shine alone. *I can partner with others.*

Dylan was a high school student, the son of my husband's tennis buddy, Bruce. One day Bruce called up Evan, clearly upset that his son had possibly joined a cult. As a child, Dylan had always been challenging. Smart. Off-the-wall energetic. Rebellious was an understatement. But recently, Bruce reported to my husband that Dylan had found Jesus through a ministry on his high school campus. Bruce concluded that this group had to be a cult—the change in Dylan was indescribable—miraculous. Bruce remembered that Evan was a Christian (I guess Evan must have let him know this somehow during their tennis outings), so he asked Evan if he and his wife could come talk to us about Dylan joining this cult.

Now I didn't really know Bruce. I'd stood in the lane next to him, timing at swim meets. I'd chatted with his wife, Belinda, at the concession stand. My main impression of him was that he was way into sports. To be honest, I don't think I'd ever have gone deeper except for his call that evening and what followed.

Bruce and Belinda rang our doorbell, and when I learned Belinda was animal allergic, I exiled our cats to the bedroom. (One very important step in evangelism is paying attention to sneezing and allergic reactions when guests come for coffee.) At our kitchen table, Bruce and Belinda described Dylan's decision to give his life to Jesus Christ. "The ministry is called Young Life. Is that a cult?" Bruce asked in earnestness.

Evan and I relaxed and launched into our own histories—his story of being raised in a Christian home and mine of similarly committing my life to Jesus through Young Life. Bruce and Belinda told us their stories. Bruce had been raised in the Catholic Church but hadn't paid much attention to faith in recent years. Belinda was more than leery of faith matters and considered herself pretty much an agnostic. At the end of the evening, Bruce asked Evan if he'd mentor Dylan in Christianity since neither Bruce nor Belinda knew much about it. Evan agreed.

Four years later, Dylan is a leader in a revival movement at his college, Bruce has committed his life to Jesus, and Belinda is watching her husband and son grow in their faith. On occasion, I've had coffee with Dylan's sister, Leanne, who is asking giant, embracing questions about Jesus, Buddha, and politics as she invests her time in caring for the Spanish-speaking poor.

Wow. All from a phone call to my husband with a plea for help.

When I look back, I'm not sure I'd have chosen to be involved were it not for Evan. I hardly knew these people. My little light seemed incredibly inadequate to make a difference. But as it happened, it wasn't my little light that God was interested in using. At least, not my little light all by itself. God's desire was that my little light join my husband's little light and that our little lights join Dylan's little light and eventually influence Bruce so that he too has a little light. Now the four of our little lights are shining before Belinda and Leanne.

The writer of Ecclesiastes speaks to the value of teamwork. In chapter 4:9–10, 12, he underlines the fact that teams provide the support, comfort, and strength required to get a job done. "Two are better than one, because they have a good return for their labor: If they fall down, they can help each other up. But pity those who fall and have no one to help them up! . . . A cord of three strands is not quickly broken."

This general Old Testament truth is expressed in the New Testament account of Jesus and the paralytic in the gospel of Mark. (I love Mark's zippy, graphic, news-reporter-style account of the ministry of Jesus.) He tells us in Mark 2 that Jesus was in a house in Capernaum, teaching to a crowd that had gathered. So many people had shown up that there was no room left, not even a spot outside the door looking in. When four men noticed that their paralyzed friend was unable to reach Jesus on his own, they got involved. They carried him to the roof, and creating an opening, they lowered him down into the presence of Jesus.

While this may sound a bit bizarre to us, in biblical times, it was a relatively simple task. Palestinian homes were constructed with an exterior stairway leading from the ground to the roof. The roofs were made of clay and mud, supported by large beams set about three feet apart. Grass grew on top of this structure. These four friends teamed together and cleverly found a way to carry their paralytic friend to Jesus. When Jesus saw the faith of these friends, and the trust of the paralytic who was lowered by them into his presence, he healed the man.

It took all four friends—each with a corner of the mat—to get their friend to Jesus. Four little lights.

I can partner. We don't have to do evangelism alone. Okay, there are moments—many of them—when our lone light alters the very nature of darkness. If we didn't go, shine, speak, or show up, darkness would prevail. But there are so many other everyday spots where we can bring our little light alongside another little light and yet another little light, together making a bright difference in the darkness.

Think through the people you know who are still on their way to Jesus, those who are paralyzed, stuck on their mats, and who can't seem to find a way to get through the door into his presence. Now, how could you partner with others who know Jesus to get these people before him?

Try gathering a group of Christian friends with a few folks who don't believe and together look at a book in the Bible (like Mark!) or watch a movie filled with Christian concepts (like *Signs* or *Bruce Almighty*). When you throw a dinner party or a barbecue, mix your guests with neighbors or co-workers. Invite a friend from church along with you for coffee with a friend from work who's searching for hope. Share your friends. Share your conversations. Share your home. Share your coffee shop. Share your neighborhood. Share your church. Share your life.

Share your faith and share your light.

Surveys of yet-to-be-believers have revealed that the majority would be somewhat likely to attend church if they were invited. (One survey reported as many as nine out of ten would go.) How many of us actually do the inviting?

Perhaps, once again, we make things harder than God intends. We don't have to do evangelism alone. *I can partner with others.* If every single person who knows Jesus has his light in them, then when we team up with each other, we increase the intensity of his light in our world. My twinkle plus your twinkle, next to his twinkle, brings a glow that's tough to ignore.

"Two are better than one, because they have a good return for their work."
....
Ecclesiastes 4:9

accept others the way they are.

be a friend.

be real.

help my children know the Jesus I know.

offer hope in the daily minutes of life.

partner with others.

I can . . . **offer help and hope in crisis.**

serve.

accept the doubts in others.

share my faith at holidays.

leave room for wonder.

keep trying even when it seems
  hopeless.

trust God with the results of my efforts.

leave a legacy of light.

"The shadow proves
the sunshine."

Jonathan Foreman

Prayers. Kisses. Lights out. I left the side of my then-nine-year-old son, Ethan's, bunk bed and started downstairs. Two steps away came, "Mom?"

Pivoting, I answered, "What, bud?"

"Mom—can you leave the bathroom light on?"

I should have expected it. He'd become obsessed with this bedtime routine. Prayers. Kisses. Lights out. Bathroom light on. But something in me resisted his request. At nine, wasn't he older than this dependency? Wasn't he big enough to go to sleep in the dark? He'd grown past the stage of boogie monsters in the closet. What was with these little-boy fears?

"Oh, Ethan—you don't need the light on anymore. You're bigger than that," I called as I continued down the stairs.

"Yes I do!" he insisted, taking matters into his own hands. "Okay. Fine. I'll turn it on myself!" he announced. Straddling the side of his bunk, he scampered to the floor and flicked the switch next door to his room. Light flooded the darkened hallway. Folding his arms across his chest, he grinned triumphantly for a minute and then returned to bed. Whatever Ethan feared, he knew clearly the remedy. Light. With a flick of a switch, he was safe. So simple.

"The LORD is my light and my salvation—whom shall I fear? The LORD is the stronghold of my life—of whom shall I be afraid?" (Ps. 27:1). Facing enemies, armies, war, destruction, false friends, David turned the darkness of his fears to the light of God. When he describes God as his light and salvation, he is expressing complete confidence that his well-being comes from the presence of God in his life. In the face of fear, light reminds him of God.

Both my son, Ethan, and the psalmist, King David, got light right. When we're afraid, light reminds us of God and his provision and protection in our dark days. Those around us, who live in darkness, are similarly attracted to light when they encounter dark moments, especially moments of crisis. They need emergency lighting, and we can offer it. Another *I can*? Yep. *I can offer help and hope to those in crisis.*

I remember visiting a friend before surgery. He wasn't especially close to God, and I knew he was nervous. I promised to stop by and see him before the operation, and I ended up praying with him, right in front of his wife who was also not so close to God. It was a tiny bit awkward at first, but after I stumbled through a question, "Would it be okay if I said a prayer for you?" and received a quiet nod, it turned out fine. I felt relieved that at least he'd had a chance to get in front of God directly before he was sedated.

In the hallway, his wife met me. "Elisa—pray with me too!" she begged through fearful and tearing eyes. I was more than surprised. Here was a woman who'd insisted she had little room for God in her life, asking me to pray for her. She was in a dark place and needed light to find her way. I prayed.

In the aftermath of the Columbine high school massacre in Colorado where I live, a friend from our MOPS International staff shared a similar experience. Her son had escaped physical harm, though the trauma he experienced from being held captive in his high school was intense. Late on the night of the tragedy, my friend found her doorbell ringing over and over as neighbor after neighbor came to their house. In the community, this family was known for their faith. Stunned and confused, a father and son, neighbors, found themselves arriving on the porch, ringing the doorbell, and requesting access to a place that seemed to offer hope in the midst of such an inexplicable horror.

My friend commented later that it was like these neighbors were moths moving toward the light of their house, unable to help themselves.

One MOPS mom wrote us saying:

> When I came to MOPS my heart was closed and it wasn't gonna open any time soon for new business! My best girlfriend had just died and I worked very hard at getting rid of all my friends so I wouldn't get hurt again. At MOPS I tried to sit by myself, but soon I was surrounded by smiles. What had I gotten myself into?? The questions flew and I shared my name and how many kids I had. The next thing I knew, I actually laughed and smiled. Over time, I made friends and my closed heart was opened.

Through his light in our lives, God offers emergency lighting to those in dark moments of crisis. Whether cancer, unemployment, floods, divorce, teen rebellion, or death, life crisis creates in people a need for hope and an openness to hear where they can find its source.

Those of us who've walked in light a long time sometimes forget this fact. Familiar with the steady beams of hope, we overlook others who are feeling their way through the darkness and are instinctively attracted to the hope we take for granted. Similarly, we who walk in light may sometimes grow indifferent to it. Stubbing a toe on life's speed bumps, we look about and wonder what we have to offer another.

It doesn't have to be complicated. Or time-consuming. Or expensive. Concrete service means much to friends in crisis who need concrete help. Offer child care to people dealing with a death in the family. Give a ride to a co-worker whose car was totaled in an accident. Leave some grocery certificates in an envelope under the doormat of a friend who becomes unemployed. Include a single mom or dad in your next social gathering; include their kids in your carpool.

Simple gestures of comfort offer hope. A card to a friend after a miscarriage. A meal to a family with a hospitalized child. A visit to a neighbor whose dog was hit by a car. Go ahead and share a book or a CD or a Scripture or a quotation that has meant something to you during a similarly painful time. Listen to God's voice prompting you to express his love for another in word or action. Be amazed at what God will do through your little light!

When people are in crisis, they crave light. All around them are dark moments of unconfirmed diagnosis, unclear decisions, unthinkable circumstances. They can't see themselves to the next minute, much less through the next step they need to take. They extend their arms blindly, wishing they'll bump into something that will help them hope themselves out of their misery.

We, who live in the light, are in the *light*. Remember, a little light goes a long way. *I can offer help and hope to those in crisis.* And even when we ourselves struggle to find our way in a moment of twilight, our twinkle is bright enough for another to find and follow.

Look, down the hall—he's keeping the light on for you and for those in your life who need to know where to turn in the darkness of crisis.

"The LORD is my light and my salvation—whom shall I fear?"
········
Psalm 27:1

accept others the way they are.

be a friend.

be real.

help my children know the Jesus I know.

offer hope in the daily minutes of life.

partner with others.

offer help and hope in crisis.

I can . . . **serve.**

accept the doubts in others.

share my faith at holidays.

leave room for wonder.

keep trying even when it seems
hopeless.

trust God with the results of my efforts.

leave a legacy of light.

"Kindness
has converted more
sinners
than zeal, eloquence, or learning."

Frederick W. Faber

W e wound our way uphill through the trees while openings in the branches above allowed the sun's lazering heat through. I could feel the sweat trickling down my back and soaking through my shirt where my daypack rested. "It's not much farther," Rich called back over his shoulder as he parted some branches and held them for me.

In rural El Salvador, I followed my guide as he snaked his way to a home visit. I had been invited to watch the work of Compassion International firsthand. Indeed, I was watching . . . and sweating . . . and amazed at the conditions so much of the world faces just to survive. For the first time in my life, I felt rich. Not just content with what I had back home in Colorado. I felt stinkin' rich.

Ahead, Rich paused at a path that forked to the right, marked only by a stack of rocks. "Okay—here's what you're going to find in just a few minutes. Oscarito is six years old. He's a Compassion-sponsored child in a family of three other children, none of whom are yet sponsored. He was being transported in a van about six months ago, when there was an accident and if it wasn't for the medical aid made possible by his sponsorship, he would have died. He's much better now, but he can't walk, and he has a tracheotomy to help him breathe. His father and mother work all day, trying to earn enough for food—his father in the fields, his mother at the market. Oscarito's two older siblings, eight and ten, also work. But his four-year-old little sister is at home with him during the day."

With that, Rich turned and set out up the path. I followed, taking care with my footing through the dog mess, the pecking chickens, and the cast-off garbage. Suddenly, before us was a shack—the stench it emitted strong and repelling. I held my breath and ducked beneath the opening as Rich had. In the darkness, I made out a rough, wooden bed, covered with a filthy, thin mattress. Atop the mattress, sitting cross-legged, a tiny little boy hissed in Spanish through the hole in his throat and suddenly broke into the sweetest smile. A sturdy beam of light rose from his face to welcome us. I'd seen precious children at every stop on this whirlwind trip through Compassion's projects in El Salvador. But this child was different. I'm not sure I've ever seen such a child since.

Attending Oscarito was an even tinier little girl. From time to time she patted Oscarito's hand, and now and then she stirred the pot of beans on the open fire in the corner of the room, shooing flies off it to do so. I was awed at the miniature caretaker he'd been assigned by family necessity.

After a fifteen-minute conversation aided by our translator, we prayed with Oscarito, hugged him and his sister, and left them to their fly-covered pot of beans and dirty mattress. My heart was full—but not with the gravity of their situation. My heart was bursting with the radiating conviction of joy that I'd just witnessed. Oscarito had no doubt—*zero*—that he was loved and adored and provided for by a loving God. He'd come to know Jesus through the Compassion project and through his stay in the hospital and through visits of folks like Rich. Unafraid, he endured his days and nights on his mattress with his baby sister as company.

The service offered by others had brought the light of hope into his dark life. Oscarito came to believe in Jesus himself because of the service of those around him.

When I consider the Oscaritos of my world, I'm humbled. I'm also a little overwhelmed. There are so many people who need help! It's easy to dismiss the homeless veteran begging at a stoplight. The government will take care of him. Or a neighborhood child who clearly needs attention from a loving adult. His mom should notice. But she's single and working a job and a half. Sure, the school has resources to intervene. But his behavior has to qualify for testing. And testing takes time.

Service can seem way too expensive for the currency of energy I have available. I think I'd rather just sponsor a child in a faraway country (actually, this is a VERY good thing to do in addition to other kinds of service) and sit on my couch with the latest reality show. Do you think I'm a creep? I am.

Here's where I need help. You probably do too. Service can make a difference in very simple forms that, once piled up, become significant.

I can serve. A cup of cold water in Jesus' name.

When Jesus talked about service in Matthew 25, he used a cup of cold water as his example. That's not too complicated. And yet a cup of cold water powerfully illustrated his love to others. "I tell you the truth, whatever you did for one of the least of these brothers of mine, you did for me" (Matt. 25:40). Faith and service are inseparable. James underlines this further in his letter, saying, "Faith by itself, if it is not accompanied by action, is dead" (2:17). Contrastingly, faith expressed in action is alive. It's visible. It communicates. Like a beam of light, it beckons others to the source. Service attracts people to Jesus. As Matthew writes in chapter 5:16, "Let your light shine before others, that they may see your good deeds and glorify your Father in heaven."

Shining service is seeing a need—and meeting it simply.

I know a woman in the Midwest who just recently started serving in a manner that has surprised even herself. Tasha began attending Kendra's church, and Kendra felt herself drawn to serve. So she committed every Monday morning to Tasha. Kendra drives to Tasha's trailer, and together they tackle a corner, or a counter, or a container. Tasha's three children ate whatever and whenever, pre-Kendra. Now they sit at a table and even use spoons.

When I marveled at her service, Kendra admitted that she has no idea how long she'll be able to sustain this sacrifice. She's a professional woman whose work demands travel and long hours of preparation. But if God wants her to continue, she'll know it's right, and so far, that's been the case.

A few weeks ago, Tasha gave her life to Jesus.

Shining service sees a need and meets it simply—and so attracts others to the source of the service.

But service doesn't just shine when it's offered from us to others. Service shines in us as we receive it as well.

One night I was speaking in a small town in west Texas. A group of women had gathered and brought their neighbors and joined together to hear about God and his hope. Good music, lots of laughter, a few words from me, and later, long conversations and many bowed heads. I was full, but weary, weary, weary.

Back in my hotel room, I slid out of my speaking clothes and into my jammies, ready for bed, when a knock came at my door. Always careful when traveling, I considered not opening the door but instead peered through the door's peephole. I recognized one of the group's committee members outside, with a bulky bag over her shoulder. I opened the door to find her smiling and lugging a giant object in a giant carrying case.

"I thought you might like a massage before bed," she responded to my raised eyebrows.

At first, I pulled back. Weird. That was my first response. But looking into her eyes, I knew that her offer was genuine, uncomplicated, and well intended. I would offend her if I refused. I widened the door and welcomed her in.

With deft actions, she began her table setup and gestured me aboard. As I lay there with her hands working the knots and aches out of my shoulders, I fought with the urge to shake away her kindness. I was fine. This felt "needy." And embarrassing. But as the lotion spread, so did the conviction that my receiving of her service was a necessary action of giving in itself.

I learned a valuable lesson that night. When we *receive* the service another offers, we *give* them the gift of meaning and value. My new friend left my hotel room beaming with the fact that she'd served me. I went to bed refreshed and filled with the peace that my reception of her gift had validated her offering.

There's a give and take in shining service. At times, we shine through service by sacrificially doing something for another. In other moments, shining through service means *receiving* what someone else needs to give.

Take a meal to a family during a hospital stay . . . and then let a friend cook for you when she offers and you're in a pinch. Include a single mom and her kids at a family celebration . . . and then say yes when she returns the invitation. Carpool more often than your "turn" calls for to cover for a traveling mom—without whining. When she thanks you for your investment, receive her gratefulness rather than brushing it off. Take your children to the nearest big box store and get stuff to fill an Operation Christmas Child shoe box for a child in a third-world country. Write a note to someone who's invested a gift in your life and thank her for what she's contributed.

In one presidential initiative, service was brought front and center through the "Thousand Points of Light" campaign. We Americans were encouraged in volunteerism: to shine our light—each of us shine our own light—knowing that when we all choose to shine through even a small point of service, our entire country is lit with hope. *I can serve.*

In the giving and receiving of service, we give and receive the love of Jesus in the everyday, up close and personal. God positively glows in us when we serve.

"Let your light shine before others, that they may see your good deeds and glorify your Father in heaven."
....
Matthew 5:16

accept others the way they are.

be a friend.

be real.

help my children know the Jesus I know.

offer hope in the daily minutes of life.

partner with others.

offer help and hope in crisis.

serve.

I can . . . **accept the doubts in others.**

share my faith at holidays.

leave room for wonder.

keep trying even when it seems
  hopeless.

trust God with the results of my efforts.

leave a legacy of light.

"He that
knows nothing
doubts nothing."

George Herbert

than and I had spent the day at the beach. The night in California had grown balmy, and backstage, where I was preparing to speak, Ethan was downing a soda. We had a good half hour before the program began, but in just minutes, a long-time family friend—who was coming to hear me for the first time—would be arriving.

I looked Ethan over. At seventeen, my son was indeed stunning. Nice slacks. Long-sleeved button shirt straight from the cleaner's bag. Dress shoes. When had I last seen him like this? Oh, yes, at a recent family funeral. This time he'd packed the clothes himself, with no prodding from me. I was impressed.

Tossing his can into the trash, he told me he'd make his way to the church foyer to wait for our friend. I stopped him and said, "Remember, I think this may be the first time in a long time she's been in a church. Please make her comfortable."

Ethan's jaw tightened, and he replied, "Well, you picked the wrong person, didn't you?"

I knew where he was headed with this comment. Ethan hadn't been in church for a while either. He was processing. You know, considering Jesus and all. It was a pretty big deal for him to accompany me, much less reach out to someone in a spiritual sense.

I took my strong son's face in my hands and responded, "No, you're just the right person to sit with her. I was there when you started out with Jesus. Even though it doesn't all make sense to you now, it does to him, and one day, you'll figure it out."

At some point in our Christian experience, most of us face the muddy waters of doubt. Whenever we encounter them, we're uncomfortable.

Doubts make us feel disloyal, even guilty. But doubts are different from unbelief. To doubt is not to reject. A doubt is an uncertainty of belief, a suspension of judgment. Doubt is a temporary attitude of questioning, whereas unbelief is a prolonged attitude that rejects something or thinks it's impossible. As we accompany others in their journeys toward God, a clear phrase can guide each of us: *I can accept the doubts in others.*

Doubting can be a necessary tool for learning. Consider the role played by doubts in your own life. Without a doubt, we'd never have a question. And without questions, we'd be without answers that cement our lives in place. We often doubt that, don't we? We shudder when God is questioned, almost afraid that he will, at last, be "found out."

God is big enough to handle doubts. As he works with us, so he works with others. He won't grow weary or find doubters disrespectful. Instead, he welcomes questions as they form yet another avenue to himself and all that he desires for people to have in him.

I love Jesus' interaction with the "doubting" disciple, Thomas. It's so honest. So accepting. When Thomas announces that he won't believe in Jesus' resurrection unless he sees it for himself, Jesus comes to him and welcomes the testing Thomas requires. Then he gently responds in John 20:29, "Because you have seen me, you have believed; blessed are those who have not seen and yet have believed." Indeed. The faith filled are blessed. At times we stand among them, utterly convinced of what we have not seen. But in other moments, what we *have* seen helps us believe in what we *haven't* seen. Ralph Waldo Emerson, though of dubious faith, said this well: "All I have seen teaches me to trust the Creator for all I have not seen."

I know a couple who struggled with naming their child "Thomas." At first they didn't want to slap him with a life label of doubt. Upon further thought, they embraced the name because it represented one who wasn't afraid to question and wasn't afraid to believe. Jesus doesn't faint in the face of weakness or frailty or doubt. Why should we?

Over coffee one afternoon, I faced a moment to apply this in real life as I met with my young friend Elana. We had been meeting now and then to talk about her spiritual interests. Elana was uncomfortable with American Christianity. Having traveled globally and witnessed poverty and need firsthand, her heart was torn and confused as to the reality of a God who would allow so much suffering. Not only did she doubt the effectiveness of the Christian faith, Elana found herself doubting the existence of the God responsible for it.

My mouth went dry for a minute as my mind searched for a response. I finally settled on mercy. Compassion. I felt Jesus' love for her and held it out to her. Tears filled my eyes, and I made it through the moment by offering her just pure emotion.

Jude 22 spells out specific instructions for how to handle the doubters among us: "Be merciful to those who doubt." Such advice raises our compassion quotient for doubters. We imagine their fear. We identify with their discomfort. We're reminded of our own unanswered questions and extend mercy in place of judgment.

All around us are flickering lights, uncertain doubters looking for proof, for help, and for truth. It's quite easy to be put off by their confusion or panic and leap into a defense of God. Rather, we are wise to sit with the tension of the apparent contradictions of our theology and to accept the lack of black and whites where we wish there were more definition.

I can accept the doubts in others.

Over the years, I've learned that tender issues often lie under the surface of doubts. Like broken trust. Racial prejudice slammed shut a heart's doorway to God when a listener heard "white only" language. Gender bias barred a woman from feeling included in a patriarchal faith. Sexual abuse from within the ranks of the church broke the bridge that a child had formed to meet the God he so desperately needed.

Or like with Ethan, beneath the cover of doubt, plain old growing up has challenged a childhood faith to take on greater meaning in the present.

As we listen and love those flickering lights in our days, we begin where people *are* rather than rushing them on to immediate change, instant commitment, or irreversible conviction. Patience is vital. Not pushing OUR agenda but sitting with God's. Standing on the steps of doubts, we listen, and in listening, we hold out the hope of God's light. In the light then, doubters can see more clearly and even make their way across what was broken to discover a new spot of stability.

Someone once said that every doubt is an assertion of faith. Leave room for doubt, that the light of faith might grow.

"Be merciful to those who doubt."
....
Jude 22

accept others the way they are.

be a friend.

be real.

help my children know the Jesus I know.

offer hope in the daily minutes of life.

partner with others.

offer help and hope in crisis.

serve.

accept the doubts in others.

I can . . . **share my faith at holidays.**

leave room for wonder.

keep trying even when it seems
  hopeless.

trust God with the results of my efforts.

leave a legacy of light.

"What I'd really like to give you
for Christmas is a star."

Ann Weems

W e took our places at the beautifully set table. Poinsettia centerpiece. Candles. Plattered slices of roast beef and serving bowls mounded with mashed potatoes and green beans. Evan and I looked across the lace tablecloth at each other. Our hosts were lovely people. We'd known them for years, yet had never had significant spiritual conversations with them. This holiday celebration was a first for our families together.

"Why don't you say your little grace?" the woman addressed my husband. Somehow, she knew that we were Christians. That grace before a meal was a custom to keep. That at Christmas, words about God needed to be voiced. It was expected, this pronouncement of the holy at the holidays. But either because she didn't know God herself, or because her faith journey was tenuous and private, she looked to us for help.

I've seen this scene replayed dozens of times at various holidays and special occasions. Christmas for sure, but also in other moments: funerals, birthdays, weddings and rehearsal dinners, Easter, even the Fourth of July. When the time comes to gather friends and/or family around a specific celebration, eyes circle the crowd and land on those of us who are plugged into a source of light to "say our little grace," offer a word of perspective, pronounce a blessing, or just do *something* faith-based. In this opening of opportunity, I'm learning *I can share my faith at holidays.*

A few guidelines have helped me learn to navigate these moments. First, expect to provide hope at the holidays. Be on the watch and vigilant for that "look" that asks for help. As when the woman turned her eyes on my husband for grace saying at her holiday meal, get ready to be asked. Sure, there's lots of controversy swirling around about the separation of church and state, but remember, we're a country that stamps "In God we trust" on our currency, places our right hand on the Holy Bible before giving testimony in court, and bows our head at funerals of co-workers we hardly even knew. Gatherings of all kinds are woven with expectations of faith expressions. Except that lots of folks participating don't know the first thing to say or do in such moments.

So go for it. Grab hands, bow heads, and talk to Jesus for them. Take along a short verse from a Psalm you could share. Be prepared with a story of how God showed up in a previous holiday. Go for it.

Second, personalize your hope at the holidays. Learn how to tell your story, personally, in the context of the holidays.

My husband, Evan, and I waited almost five years to become parents. When we married, we knew that we wouldn't be able to have children biologically. We'd determined that we would adopt. To be honest, at first I was uncertain if I really wanted to be a mother. My own family had been broken and bruised early, leaving me in the caretaking role. My heart hesitated at the thought of mothering "again."

At first.

Years passed—full years as a married couple without children, filled to the brim with fun, friends, service, and each other. Our names came off the "inactive" waiting list onto the "active" waiting list at the adoption agency. My heart stirred at the thought of a baby—my own child. As if a timer beeped, I was ready. I wanted to be a mother. More than anything.

Another year passed. And another. At this point, time passed painfully, ploddingly, slooooowwwwly. Everyone else was pregnant or mothering. When invitations to baby showers appeared in my mailbox, I shuddered at the thought of all the pink and blue, the oooohhhs and aaaaahhhs. Eventually I'd just send a gift and stay home. Mother's Day was the worst. When the minister asked the moms to stand and directed the ushers to welcome them with carnations. I wanted to slide under the pew and slither out into the foyer.

Christmastime came. I had to do something. My mother-in-law had won an artificial Christmas tree at some event and shipped it to me. I set it up in a corner of our living room (our *real* tree was in the family room), stuffed baby's breath in the gaps, and tied pink and blue satin ribbons on the branches. Each morning I'd stop at that tree and pray, "Oh, God, please. Please give us a baby by Christmas." The tree became a tangible symbol of our wait, a gesture of promise. I christened it the "Hope for the Baby Tree."

Three days before Christmas, the phone rang, and I was informed that the only other waiting couple in our group who hadn't yet received a baby had one. I called my caseworker. She said there was no way we'd have a baby by Christmas. I felt as if I'd been shot in the chest. My knees collapsed under me, and I sank to the ground, receiver in hand. I, who'd never really wanted to be a mother, I WANTED A BABY!

After the holidays, I stubbornly left up the Hope for the Baby Tree in the living room. But finally in February, I took it down, aware of the neighbors' guarded glances. I'd thunk the mattress on the baby crib we'd set up in our waiting nursery. Dust would fly.

Easter weekend approached. I sat on my sofa, bunny slippers tucked under me while a blizzard raged outside on the streets of Denver. The phone rang, and our caseworker spoke the words I'd longed to hear for so long. "You have a daughter!"

The next day in church, Evan and I stood with tears streaming down our cheeks, singing, "Jesus Christ is risen today!" Indeed. Hope rose in my heart as well. I had a daughter. Eva was at last real. Twenty-eight months later our son, Ethan, joined our family, only thirteen days old.

Every Christmas—from the waiting one to today's—we set up a Hope for the Baby Tree, and with its pink- and blue-edged symbol as background, we share the story of our faith journey to becoming a family with children to all who ask. We also talk about Jesus' birthday. As we unpack the decorations for the season, a bright and shiny methodology emerges from the storage box: *I can share my faith at holidays.* It's as natural as telling my family history or the story of my children's arrival into our family.

Third, enlarge your view of the "holidays." While it might be the most expected season for shining, Christmas isn't the only holiday when faith can be shared. I know some families who roll their faith stories out on New Year's as they think a bit about the worst and best from last year and the worst and best yet to be discovered in the year to come. A long-married friend of mine partners with her husband to create a lavish dinner of pampering for their single women friends on Valentine's Day. These women—whether single through divorce, death, or career single-ness—enjoy a meaningful dinner with others on a day typically set apart for romance and so discover the true Romancer of their soul . . . Jesus.

Here's the deal: people love holidays and are game to celebrate them all. Who doesn't like a party? Plus they're open to knowing the origins of the holidays—what they mean and where they came from.

A few millennia ago, God expressed the birth of the Messiah with a star. That star led the shepherds and the Magi to meet Jesus, the Son of God, the Christ. Asking, "Where is the one who has been born king of the Jews? We saw his star in the east and have come to worship him" (Matt. 2:2), the Magi approached Herod for information. The star led them to Jesus.

At Christmas, Valentine's, and the Fourth of July, God's people offer light to those wanting desperately to know a real reason to celebrate. *I can share my faith at the holidays.* When the conversation stops and turns to those of us who have followed God's star to his Son, we can shine.

"Where is the one who has been born king of the Jews?

We saw his star in the east and have come to worship him."
....
Matthew 2:2

accept others the way they are.

be a friend.

be real.

help my children know the Jesus I know.

offer hope in the daily minutes of life.

partner with others.

offer help and hope in crisis.

serve.

accept the doubts in others.

share my faith at holidays.

I can . . . **leave room for wonder.**

keep trying even when it seems
  hopeless.

trust God with the results of my efforts.

leave a legacy of light.

"Wonder is the basis of worship."

Thomas Carlyle

I was standing in church in the forming line, where everyone prepared to take communion. This practice of standing, walking, and approaching a communion station was new to me. The custom of my previous church was to sit in the pew and pass the elements. But I was visiting a new church, and the pastor directed us to stand and go to God, so to speak.

The overhead lights in the movie-theater-turned-sanctuary were dimmed, and the communion stations, simple tables laden with a plate of crackers and a goblet of grape juice, were spotlighted. Banners with bright colors declaring messages like "Alleluia" and "Rejoice" hung above each station.

I followed my row out of my pew, placing my son, Ethan, then about seven years old, just ahead of me. I kept my hands reassuringly on his shoulders, knowing this practice was new to him as well. As we arrived and stopped at the station, we watched the people ahead of us and then modeled our actions after their example. Pick up the cracker. Dip it in the cup of juice. Place it on our tongues. Turn and head back to the pew.

Soft music accompanied the pastor as he recited Jesus' entire prayer for his disciples from John 17. He knew it by heart. Another element in a long line of impressive moments. Back in our pew, Ethan looked up at me. "Wow. That was *dramatic*," he said, raising his eyebrows.

When we're knee-deep in the wonder of worship, God unexpectedly and inexplicably reveals the sacredness of his being. Wonder. Mystery. Drama. An experience beyond ourselves and our comprehension. There are many among us who become convinced of Christ when they are most aware of his "otherness." Think of Moses at the burning bush. Or Paul on the road to Damascus. Or Mary startled by an angel of God telling her she would give birth to the Messiah.

Okay—maybe we don't run into such Cecil B. DeMille moments of the miraculous in *our* everyday. But the sacred still approaches, beckoning our attention and guiding our gaze. In sharing our faith with others, we're wise to resist the urge to explain and instead to leave room for the mystery. To explore rather than answer. Another *I can* for those of us choosing to twinkle: *I can leave room for wonder.*

"Twinkle, twinkle, little star, how I wonder what you are. Up above the world so high, like a diamond in the sky." Just as the diamond brilliance of a star in the inky sky draws our eye to wonder about the universe beyond, so does the mysterious experience of God lead others to ponder his essence. *How I wonder what you are. Up above the world so high.*

Last summer our family took a kind of "divide and conquer" weekend away. My husband went one direction with our grown daughter and grandson, and I went another with Ethan and his then-girlfriend, Kiley. Different stages, different needs. You know the story. By this time, Ethan was eighteen—a grown-up guy compared to the seven-year-old wonderer of years ago. Kiley had been in our lives for several years, and thus our conversation over dinner on a Colorado mountainside was stressless, but routine and bordering on boring.

I decided to stir things up. In this season of his life, Ethan was processing God and what he thought of him. I wondered where he was with God—and where Kiley was too. So I invented a conversation game. Here were the rules: Together we named five topics (everyone got to offer a suggestion). Then each person picked one of the five to lead by asking a question everyone had to answer. (This narrowed the five down to three remaining topics.) For each topic, a second person also got to ask a follow-up question for all to answer before we went on to the next topic.

Our five nominated topics ended up being memories, nature, dreams, religion, and current events. Ethan picked memories. Kiley picked dreams. I picked religion (of course!).

Here's what we ended up with in terms of questions:

Memories

Lead Question: What is your favorite memory of your childhood?

Follow-up Question: What do you wish your child's best memory would be?

Dreams

Lead Question: Where do you want to be in five years?

Follow-up Question: Five years ago, where did you think you'd be now?

Religion

Lead Question: When did you feel closest to God?

Follow-up Question: When did you feel furthest from God?

The answers were fascinating. Theirs, mine, and ours. I learned about their fears and wounds and joys, and I shared both familiar and new realizations of my own. In such a discussion, there was room for pondering, for curiosity, and for vulnerability. We left room for the mystery of discovering each other and—in that process—more of who God is, who he wants us to be, and what he wants us to have in him. Together, we wondered.

"That was dramatic." While Ethan didn't put his feelings into those exact words this time, I recognized the response in my son's eyes. Jesus had just visited our dinner table and left us in the wake of his presence.

Now I'm not the only one who's ever thought of using questions to spark interest in spiritual things. Ha! Several popular family games use this concept. More importantly, it was a central practice of Jesus himself: picking up a cue from the culture and engaging his listeners with a question in response. When Peter asked for "closure" on the identity of Jesus, the question, "Whom do you say that I am?" became his answer. "Why are you afraid?" to the disciples in the storm at sea. "How many loaves do you have?" to the disciples tasked with feeding the five thousand. "Why do you call me good?" to the rich young ruler. "What do you want me to do for you?" to blind Bartimaeus. On and on came the questions, but more often than not the answers were vague, open, and filled with more questions. Further and further came the understanding that in the presence of Jesus was mystery.

Questions are crucial tools for evangelism. They offer suggestions and open-ended options for consideration. They are invitations to move from monologue to dialogue. Questions are fitting rooms for the values and philosophies that may become the wardrobe of personal commitments.

That is, if we ask them minus the trappings of pigeonholed answers. Sans black-and-white, know-it-all assumptions. Without formulas. With room for wonder.

The prophet Isaiah mulls over the mystery of God's nature in the very famous chapter 40 of his work, asking, "Who has understood the mind of the LORD?" in verse 13. It is this very mystery and wonder that he further illustrates in verses 25–26, where he continues, "'To whom will you compare me? Or who is my equal?' says the Holy One. Lift your eyes and look to the heavens: Who created all these? He who brings out the starry host one by one, and calls them each by name."

I can leave room for wonder. Whether it's a moment in church worship, a mountain hillside dinner on a Colorado summer evening, or a conversation over lattes, leave room for God's mysterious ways. There is reverence in the asking. *How I wonder what you are.*

"Who has understood the mind of the Lord?"
....
Isaiah 40:13

accept others the way they are.

be a friend.

be real.

help my children know the Jesus I know.

offer hope in the daily minutes of life.

partner with others.

offer help and hope in crisis.

serve.

accept the doubts in others.

share my faith at holidays.

leave room for wonder.

I can . . . **keep trying even when it seems hopeless.**

trust God with the results of my efforts.

leave a legacy of light.

"This is my quest,
to follow that star,
no matter how hopeless,
no matter how far . . .
to reach
the unreachable star."

Joe Darion, Man of La Mancha

After my conversion experience with Young Life, I became very zealous about others around me also asking Jesus into their hearts and becoming Christians. One of my leaders encouraged me to formulate what she called a "Most Wanted" list and on it to write the names of those I'd most like to see come to Christ. Then I was supposed to pray for them and—gulp—talk to them.

So I grabbed the nearest spiral notebook and started writing. I didn't make it much past my family, since as far as I could see, there were plenty of yet-to-be-believers right within the walls of my home.

My younger brother was quick to respond. He liked the idea of God. Turned out my older sister had walked a journey similar to mine and had formalized her young Presbyterian church faith through Young Life a few years prior. Due to the fact that my dad lived thousands of miles away from our home in Houston, I rarely saw him in those days, so he didn't even make my list. (I kind of cringe at the omission now.)

At the top of my "Most Wanted" list was my mother—Paige—and she remained there for most of my life. Paige used to say that at the age of twelve, she walked down the aisle of a little Baptist church in a small town in Texas and gave her life to Jesus. I never saw a trace of her faith in her life. (Well, maybe she *did* drive my sister and me to church as children—but why did she just drop us off and leave? Why didn't she stay?)

Perhaps I wasn't looking. . . .

Paige was a bright, gifted, petite woman who forayed into broadcasting in her early twenties in New York City. Coming from Fort Worth, Texas, and being a woman in the 1940s, this was a feat. As a child, she survived polio—another amazing accomplishment. When she was a young woman, her fiancé was killed tragically, and she survived to love again. She married my father when she was twenty-six, quit her broadcasting job, and joined him in many moves around the country as he worked his own broadcasting career to success.

After nine years and three children, they were divorced. My mother was an alcoholic then. Her drinking colored my days as a child, a teenager, and a young adult with a topaz glow. Late at night, she'd pinball down the hall of our ranch-style home, bumping into one wall and then the other, glass of scotch in hand. She continued to drink until she died.

My mother meant well. She set out to be a good mom. She decorated holidays with lavish gifts and celebrations. Her humor was dry and witty. Creating snacks christened "pinnemickles" from frozen pineapple chunks pierced with a toothpick, she entertained us and our friends. But come five o'clock—on the weekends it was noon—her love turned into what wasn't safe as she screwed the top off the bottle of scotch. She became unpredictable. Sloppy. Confused and confusing. As she left a vacuum of leadership in our home, I slipped into the gap, caring for my brother, cleaning the house, making the meals, and waking my mother up on weekdays so she could get to work.

So . . . when my mom testified of her early faith as a twelve-year-old, I scrunched up my brain and tried to imagine how, if she loved Jesus, she could continue to show so little evidence of his character in her habits.

It's not that I didn't want my mom to become a Christian. Mercy—I'd have given anything if she had discovered the hope I'd found in Jesus. I prayed for her constantly. I talked with her about God. At first, she thought I'd become a freak. She asked, "Why did you have to become a Christian? Haven't you always known God?" Then she remembered her Baptist church moment and eagerly held it out for my approval as if to say, "Does this count?" But to me it didn't. Because to me her life hadn't looked different as a result of that walk down the aisle.

My prayers for her continued even as I grew up and away. From time to time, I'd tell her again of my concern for her and her life and of the love God had for her. Response: zip. To me, my mom was an unreachable star. An impossible dream.

Most of us have such souls on our "Most Wanted" lists. People we love, or want to love. Irregular people. Unsafe people. People in need of hope and help who don't seem to know they are in need of hope and help. Occasionally we reach a moment of joy when we pick up a pencil and can actually draw a line through a name, leaping with relief and ecstasy at their journey from darkness to light. More often than seems to fit with the promise of our faith, our list yellows and curls on our refrigerator door, mocking our prayers, ridiculing our honest utterances of hope.

What do we do then? I'll tell you but not without stuttering. It's taken me longer than most to learn this *I can*, but I do believe it. *I can keep trying even when it seems hopeless.*

When I was in my thirties and my mother neared the end of her sixties, she was diagnosed with cancer. I was stunned, like any daughter. But on the other side of my surprise, panic attacked me. The clock ticked noisily. I felt a heavy burden for her eternity, and yet my heart hardened and grew hopeless, loveless, and prayerless. There were just so many holes in my heart from her "unlove" in my life. What more could I do than I'd already done?

Very quickly the answer came: I could enlist help. Two stars are brighter than one. I turned to my friend Bonnie, my mother's age and many times over my mentor in all things spiritual. I asked Bonnie to pray for my mother because I couldn't. Gladly, she agreed, but she wanted to know just what I wanted her to pray for. I asked her to please pray for my mother to see her need for God and to desire heaven. I waited. Bonnie prayed.

The week my mother died, she called to tell me that she'd remembered two poems, both spiritual in nature. One was "L'Envoi" by Rudyard

Kipling—all about heaven. The other was "Footprints in the Sand." For some reason, she said, she felt I needed to know this.

I flew to her bedside, along with my older sister and younger brother, and there we took turns tending to my mother as she lingered in and out of consciousness. One afternoon, from the foot of her hospital bed, I watched as my sister sat near her head and my mother seemed to look "through her." An odd moment, but I chalked it up to the angle of where I was sitting. But when it was my time to rotate to the position by her head, I noticed that indeed, she wasn't looking *at* me but rather to my right. So, I shifted my body over to make it easier for her to see my face. After all, I was sure she'd want to gaze at the face of her dear daughter.

With willowy arms, she reached out and pushed me gently back in place, extending her hands into the empty space she'd created next to me.

I moved again. She pushed me back again. I looked into her eyes. She looked to my side. I asked, "Mother, do you *see* something here?"

"Yes, Elisa. I see Jesus," my mother replied.

My mother, who had walked the aisle as a twelve-year-old to give her life to Jesus and then had apparently taken it back for the remaining fifty years, was holding on to Jesus as her life slipped away from here into eternity.

My mother completed her walk into the arms of Christ in 1991. Drilled into my being is a principle of evangelism that I pray will never leave me. Don't give up. Ever. Unreachable stars are still within God's grasp.

In 2 Peter 3:8–9, we're oriented to God's perspective of time by these words: "But do not forget this one thing, dear friends: With the Lord a day is like a thousand years, and a thousand years are like a day. The Lord is not slow in keeping his promise, as some understand slowness. He is patient with you, not wanting anyone to perish, but everyone to come to repentance."

Who is the unreachable star on your "Most Wanted" list? Take the hard step to ask for help in reaching him or her. Two stars are brighter than one. And then, never give up. Not ever. *I can keep trying even when it seems hopeless.* No star, no matter how hopeless, no matter how far, is beyond the grasp of God.

After packing up my mother's belongings, holding her memorial service, and returning home to Colorado, I was driving to the store when I glanced up through the windshield to the blue, cloud-speckled sky. The realization rippled through me: "You can *see* me now, can't you, Mother? You can *love* me now." I smiled. Now that was worth waiting for.

P.S. Now, lest you grow jealous and finicky, not all of my "Most Wanteds" have had such a clear response. Read on to the next chapter. . . .

"He is patient with you, not wanting anyone to perish,

but everyone to come to repentance."

. . . .

2 Peter 3:9

accept others the way they are.

be a friend.

be real.

help my children know the Jesus I know.

offer hope in the daily minutes of life.

partner with others.

offer help and hope in crisis.

serve.

accept the doubts in others.

share my faith at holidays.

leave room for wonder.

keep trying even when it seems
hopeless.

I can . . . **trust God with the results of my efforts.**

leave a legacy of light.

"What about the person you know who as far as you can possibly tell has never had such a moment—the sore-heads and slobs of the world, the ones the world has hopelessly crippled? Maybe for that person the moment that has to happen is you."

Frederick Buechner

My father died, and I don't know where he is.

When I was a skinny, dirty-kneed five-year-old, my parents divorced. My older sister, younger brother, and I moved with my mother to the San Francisco Bay area. My father moved to Miami and remarried soon thereafter. About once a year, my sister and I wore dresses tied with sashes at our young waists, uncurled our hair from the bobby pins my mother had carefully inserted, and waited at the window with our matching purses for my father to pull up in a sleek car to take us to dinner.

Those evenings were always tense. We clutched fork and knife, sawing away at our steaks while our legs dangled from adult-sized chairs. As a preteen, I remember practicing conversation pointers in advance. "What do you think of Jimmy Carter, Daddy?" "Do you think college is a good idea for a girl?" My father was always kind, always patient, and always answered these questions. But he didn't know much about little girls, and as the years passed, a greater and greater distance grew between us that no conversation seemed able to bridge.

Not long after I clarified what I thought about God and Jesus as a teenager, my mother and I had an argument about my father and the fact that he'd always been so distant from me. I hollered, "I don't even really have a father!" to which she responded, "Oh, yes you do, and he loves you very much." (Even though my parents had split up under the normal devastation of divorce, I have to credit my mother with never bad-mouthing my father. She always held him up to us with respect. Yea Paige!)

The night of this fight, I had a dream. I was high atop a cliff, looking down into a deep crevice, when suddenly I fell. Careening down toward the sharp, flesh-colored rocks below, I felt I'd surely die, my body smashed when I hit their surface. To my surprise, I found myself not landing on sharp rocks but rather cradled, in the soft palms of hands. A voice gently announced, "I am your heavenly Father. I will never leave you or forsake you." I awoke aware of my earthly father's love and newly convinced of my heavenly Father's care.

Several years later, I put my dad on my "Most Wanted" list. That took courage. Any time I broached the subject of religion, he'd change it. And it took effort for us to find time to get together. He still lived in the southeast, and I'd moved to Colorado. In one visit, a late-night hot tub conversation, my father told me he was a "self-made" man and that he didn't like the whole concept of needing God. This made sense because he'd been on his own since his own father walked out when he was about seven. But it hurt my heart.

Over the next decade or so, my dad and I forged a nice relationship. He and my stepmom loved on my babies as they arrived. We were invited to visit, and the invitation was returned. Then, as my father aged and began to fail, I found my heart drawn even more intensely to him. I joined my stepmother for his first and second open-heart surgeries and prayed with them before both. In one moment of recovery, my father actually "died," and the medical team brought him back. In recovery he told me he could hear voices saying, "He's gone!"

That got me. When my father returned home and I flew back to Colorado, I composed a letter telling my dad how much I loved him. I wrote, "Dad, when I next hear the words, 'He's gone!' I want to know where it is you've gone. I've spent so much of my life without you. I long to spend the hereafter with you." I inserted a picture of me with him and mailed it.

A few weeks later, my father moved home to die. I flew to his side, as did my siblings. I whispered prayers in his ear. I held his hand. When he took his last breath, my stepmother, their daughter, and I were together at his side. In and out, he breathed. In and out. In and out. He was gone.

And I still didn't know where. A black hole. An unknowable place without definition. Astronomers identify black holes as a certain variety of celestial graveyard, holding the fate of some stars . . . collapsing indefinitely, leaving only a source of gravity so strong that even light cannot escape from it.

Late that night, after reminiscing my father's life with the rest of the family, I sat alone on my bed, stunned. Just six years before, I'd *watched* my mother slip from life to death *holding Jesus' hand.* Though she was seemingly an unreachable star, God had grabbed her and led her firmly home. What was the deal with my dad? Why didn't God do it again? Maybe not in the same way. Okay. But still—why didn't he do something to show me where my dad had gone?

When Peter wrote to first-century believers who were being persecuted for their faith, he encouraged them to follow Jesus' example in how they handled suffering. In 1 Peter 2:23, we're told, "When they hurled their insults at him, he did not retaliate; when he suffered, he made no threats. Instead, he entrusted himself to him who judges justly."

This is the Scripture God used to comfort me, months after my father's death when still I wrestled with God's ways. If I truly believed that God is the gracious and holy judge of all, would I trust him to judge my father justly? Not easily. Not every minute. Not without a few doubts here and there. But would I?

Just what does that mean? In Hebrews 4:13 we're told that nothing is hidden from God's eyes—that all is laid bare before him—the one to whom we will one day give account. From where I sat with my dad, I couldn't *see* his decision. But the all-seeing God wasn't blinded as to the thoughts and intentions of my dad's heart. God would deal with what he saw according to my dad's character.

Here lies the most yielded of all the *I cans*. *I can trust God with the results of my efforts.*

I think of the parable of the man who worked for a day and the one who worked for an hour in Matthew 20. Each was paid the same. That's tough to swallow—that if you've been following God since a child and if you just decided to align with him on your last breath, you get the same result: heaven. But I've come to accept it. Sin is sin. Bad stuff. All needing forgiveness equally. Only a great judge—fair and merciful—can deliver such forgiveness when it's requested.

Would I trust this kind of judge? Yes . . . I believe that God sees all and judges justly. So I relinquished my father into his hands.

We can love people enough to write their names on our "Most Wanted" lists. We can love these people and tell them of the hope we have in Jesus and how they can have it too. We can tell them we want to know where they've gone when we hear the words, "She's gone!" That's what we can do. That's what we need to do.

But when we don't know how someone has responded to the truth we have shared, we can trust the Judge who judges justly. *I can trust God with the results of my efforts.*

"He entrusted himself to him who judges justly."
. . . .
1 Peter 2:23

accept others the way they are.

be a friend.

be real.

help my children know the Jesus I know.

offer hope in the daily minutes of life.

partner with others.

offer help and hope in crisis.

serve.

accept the doubts in others.

share my faith at holidays.

leave room for wonder.

keep trying even when it seems
hopeless.

trust God with the results of my efforts.

I can . . . **leave a legacy of light.**

"We do not truly see light,
we only see slower things lit by it."

C. S. Lewis

Light isn't just about today. Light can be about tomorrow too. When we shine like stars in the universe, we can leave a legacy of light, lighting the way home for others who come behind us.

In Ephesians 5:8, Paul writes, "For you were once darkness, but now you are light in the Lord. Live as children of light." Doesn't that grab you? "You *were* once darkness, but now you *are* light"! This is Paul's hope for us—Jesus' desire for our days—that our lives will tell our story, and point to our hope, long after we've lived them.

More than a century ago, a man named John Todd wrote a letter to encourage an aunt who was dying. To soothe her anxieties, he reminded her of the way she took him in when the death of his parents left him orphaned.

My Dear Aunt—

I am sorry to hear that you are feeble, perhaps I should say sick, and even that there is fear on your part that you are not to be better in this world. . . .

You remember that it is now thirty-five years since my father died, and left me, a little boy six years old, without a mother, without a home, and with nobody to care for me. It was then that you sent word that you would take me and give me a home, and be as a mother to me. . . . At length the day was set when I was to go to you, ten miles off. What a long journey it seemed to me! And I well remember how disappointed I was that, instead of coming for me yourself, you sent old Caesar, the great fat, black man, to bring me to you. How my heart sunk when he came, and I was told that I was to ride on the horse behind him, sitting on the blanket! ... So we set out, just before night. Caesar took my bundle of clothing before him, and (my little dog) ran beside us. But long before we got to your house, I began to feel tired, my legs ached, and I was tired of taking hold of Caesar. By-and-by the evening and the darkness came on, and I felt afraid.... Caesar, too, was so dark that I could not see him, and he jogged on without saying a word. He had no idea that I was afraid.

"Caesar, ain't we most there?" said I in my terror.

"Yes, when we have got through these woods we shall see the candle in the house."

"Won't they be gone to bed?" for it seemed to me it must be nearly morning.

"Oh no, they will be all ready to receive us."

But at last, after winding and turning and going uphill and downhill, a long, long way, as it seemed to me, we came out of the woods, and then the stars shone; and I was told which light was in your house. And when we got there you came out, and you gently took me in your arms as Caesar handed me down; and you called me your "poor little boy," and you led me gently in; and there was the blazing, warm fire, the bright light, and the table spread, and the supper all waiting for me! ... How you soothed me and warmed me and put me to bed in the strange room, and heard me say my prayers, and stayed with me till I was fast asleep!

And now, my dear aunt, you see why I have recalled all this to your memory. Your heavenly Father will send for you—a dark messenger it may be. And he will be your conductor, and carry you safely through the darkness of the way. He will not drop nor leave you, for he is a faithful servant. You need not feel afraid, for he knows the way, and will take you directly to your home. There the door will be open, and your dearest friend, the Lord Jesus Christ, will meet you and take you in, and the light and glory of his presence all seen. What a welcome you will receive!

At any rate, don't fear the dark passage, nor the dark messenger. Receive it all as the little child did, and you will find the home.

Ever, ever yours, most gratefully,

John Todd.[1]

Finding home. It's what we want for ourselves. It's what we want for all those we love. God lights the way home for others through his light in us.

Sometimes I daydream about the future. I mean the WAY future: the nursing home. I picture myself depleted and most likely compromised in my abilities. But I'm prepared. I have a box where I save cards, emails, tiny gifts of encouragement that whisper from Jesus, "Yes, my child. I used you in this person's life. Your twinkle shed my light along the way." I plan to pull out that box and make my way through it as often as possible, buoyed by the messages of hope contained there.

I can leave a legacy of light. We can get past the *I can'ts.* We can grab on to the *I cans.*

Twinkle, twinkle, little star. Share your faith . . . one light at a time.

"For you were once darkness, but now you are light
in the Lord. Live as children of light."
. . . .
Ephesians 5:8

1. John E. Todd, ed., *John Todd: The Story of His Life* (New York: Harper and Brothers, 1876), 35–37.

Twinkle Questions

This Little Light of Mine

1. Why did you pick up this book? In other words, what is your greatest felt-need regarding evangelism?
2. We've identified the *I can'ts* of sharing our faith in seven objections. Rank these for yourself, beginning with your top *I can't* down to your bottom one.
3. How does the concept that one speck of light changes the nature of darkness influence your feelings about evangelism? Do you agree that God wouldn't ask us to participate in something that is impossible?

Chapter One: I can't . . . I have such a small light.

1. Label your light. What do you like about your light? What aspects are hard for you to accept? How can you embrace both the strengths and the possible weaknesses of your light label?
2. Looking at the light you are, where could you direct it? How could you do this?

3. Everyone endures "night times" in life. Describe a dark season you have survived. Where/how did you find light to make your way through?

Chapter Two: I can't . . . I might fail.

1. How does seeing God as responsible for light and you as responsible for your candle move you to adjust your approach?
2. In order to be lit, an unlit candle must bow to a lit candle. If a lit candle chases an unlit candle, it may spill wax and perhaps blow itself out in the hustle. Who are you chasing with your candle?
3. If you're responsible for your candle, what action do you need to take to stay lit?

Chapter Three: I can't . . . I don't want to get involved.

1. People can be a lot of trouble. It's just honest to admit this. But sometimes the trouble we assume in others is of our own making. How do you pull back from getting involved with others who might need your faith because you assume they wouldn't be interested?
2. Can you label someone in your life who is like the Carters were in mine—someone you've decided wouldn't be interested just because of how you evaluate the externals of his or her life?
3. Sit with the Scripture from this chapter for a minute: "Who was I to think that I could oppose God?" (Acts 11:17). God stunned Peter with wanting the Gentiles to be in a relationship with him. Is there someone you are opposing coming to Christ? What would it mean for you to stop your opposition?

Chapter Four: I can't . . . I don't want to offend.

1. How do you "hide" your faith?
2. From whom do you "hide" your faith? Why?
3. What would be a first step for you to take to illuminate rather than eliminate in this situation?

Chapter Five: I can't . . . I don't have a dramatic story to tell.

1. What's your excuse for not wanting to tell your story? It's boring? It's too dramatic? You don't know how? Identify what holds you back.
2. Select one of the chapter's suggestions for developing your story and do it.
3. Make a list of "Christianese" phrases you tend to use without thinking and determine to drop them from your story vocabulary. (Examples to get you started: "what a blessing!"; "quiet time"; "my walk with God.")

Chapter Six: I can't . . . I don't know all the answers.

1. What do you know that you know that you know?
2. How do you know this?
3. Other than the Bible, what source could you use to share what you know?

Chapter Seven: I can't . . . I don't know how to relate to people who aren't like me.

1. Have you ever found yourself in a discussion about your faith and encountered accusations that Christians are arrogant, judgmental, or narrow? How did you handle that moment? Would you respond differently after having read this chapter?
2. Imagine sharing your faith story with someone in the generation above you, like your mom or dad. Based on this chapter, what tack would you take? How would you change tactics for other audiences beside or below you?
3. How much can a container change to give light to the culture without altering the light itself?

From Darkness to Light

1. Describe the process of your conversion. What people and forces did God use to move you from darkness to light?
2. Having stopped to think about your conversion in light of the processes of God, do you have any new insights?

Chapter Eight: I can . . . accept others the way they are.

1. Make a list of the no-no's you tend to impose on others. Now take a look at your list. Would Jesus include such items on such a list?
2. Are there certain types or categories of people whom you tend to impose your no-no list upon? Children, adolescents, family, subcultures?
3. Sometimes we create no-no lists out of fear. Take a look in your heart . . . is fear motivating your no-no screen? What are you afraid of?

Chapter Nine: I can . . . be a friend.

1. Does belonging *always* come before believing? What might be some exceptions to this general principle?
2. Think back to your own journey to Jesus. In what way did you belong before you believed?
3. Who is God bringing into your days, inviting her or him to "belong to you"? What barriers might you be throwing up to avoid intimacy? Have you swallowed the lie that independence is more mature than intimacy? Where do you need to "head back to Texas" in your thinking?

Chapter Ten: I can . . . be real.

1. Has God been vulnerable to you? What can you learn from his example?
2. What is the difference between being vulnerable and parading your faults?
3. Who is watching you who needs to see you model the process of your faith?

Chapter Eleven: I can . . . help my children know the Jesus I know.

1. Do you believe that children can know God? What does their faith look like compared to the faith of adults?
2. If you have young children, what "tiny twinkle" helps might you choose to incorporate into your family?
3. If you have grown children, what "take away" is God giving you from this chapter for your children's faith journey?

Chapter Twelve: I can . . . offer hope in the daily minutes of life.

1. Can you identify a regular, everyday moment when God brought you an opportunity to be a "shooting star" to someone? How did you respond initially?

2. What barriers do you tend to throw up to such stray moments in your days? Why? How can you open yourself up without dropping protective and wise barriers altogether?

3. Have you ever been given an opportunity to directly lead someone to Jesus? When you face an opportunity to "close the deal," how do you respond?

Chapter Thirteen: I can . . . partner with others.

1. Many of us pull back at the thought of partnering to share our faith with others. We'd rather do things on our own, in our own timing, and at our own pace. Can you identify such resistance in yourself? What might you be missing with this "lone ranger" attitude?

2. Think through people you know who need Jesus. Can you identify barriers that make it difficult for them to get into his presence? (These might include past experiences with Christianity or the church, or friends and family issues, and so on.) How might you help them get past these barriers? Do you know a friend who might come alongside you to help in the process?

3. Sometimes we actually have to pull back from being "in charge" so that others can get involved in helping someone come to Christ. Is there something you need to stop doing so that others can partner with you in this process?

Chapter Fourteen: I can . . . offer help and hope in crisis.

1. Think of a time when you faced a crisis yourself. In what person or source did light appear to offer you hope?

2. Remember a moment when you came upon someone in a dark crisis needing emergency lighting. How did you make a difference in this situation? Can you see any lasting result from your assistance as you look back over time?

3. The very definition of the word *crisis* implies the unexpected. How can you prepare yourself for a twinkling response when you next face the need for emergency lighting?

Chapter Fifteen: I can . . . serve.

1. There are times for all of us when service comes easily. In fact, we can "lose" ourselves in service to others. Describe a situation when service came easily to you. What difference did your service make in the lives around you?

2. There are other times when we feel compelled to serve, but we don't really want to. It's too much trouble. We're uncomfortable. Excuses bubble up and warn us not to get involved. Can you think of such a moment? How did you respond?

3. In this chapter, the concept is raised that *receiving* service from another person actually *gives* them the gift of being able to invest their offering. From whom do you need to receive service so that he or she might enjoy the gift of giving?

Chapter Sixteen: I can . . . accept the doubts in others.

1. In what areas of your faith do you doubt? Not sure? Don't just listen to a sermon in church. Follow the text in your own Bible.

Do you believe that the preacher is accurately interpreting the passage?

2. Start a journal and in it record your ponderings regarding life, how God works, and the especially "hard stuff" of illness, suffering, and so on.

3. The next time someone "doubts," pay attention to your own response. What are you tempted to say or do in response? Why?

Chapter Seventeen: I can . . . share my faith at holidays.

1. Can you think of a time when "all eyes" landed on you at a holiday celebration? What was your response? Looking back, is there anything you would have done differently?

2. Take one holiday—perhaps Christmas. How can you personalize your faith story for this setting?

3. Think through the holidays coming up on the calendar. How might you share your faith on one particular occasion?

Chapter Eighteen: I can . . . leave room for wonder.

1. Describe a time when you encountered what you would call the "mystery" of God. Where were you? What happened? How did this experience affect your faith?

2. When you sit with the fact that we can't and won't know everything about God and faith in his Son, Jesus, what emotions rise up in you? Is there tension created? Why do you think this might happen?

3. As you process the use of questions in accessing the wonder of God, what principles can you list as to what makes a good question and what makes a less than desirable question?

Chapter Nineteen: I can . . . keep trying even when it seems hopeless.

1. Do you have a "Most Wanted" list? If not, are you interested in creating one? If so, whose names would you include?
2. Name an "unreachable star" in your life today. Now, whom could you invite alongside to brighten your glow before him or her?
3. At times it seems that God is incredibly slow at responding to our prayers for others. How do his sovereignty and our free will help you adjust your patience? What feelings do you experience when you consider that one who accepts Jesus at death is as present in God's eternal kingdom as one who comes to know him as a child? What does the Bible say about this reality in Matthew 20:1–16?

Chapter Twenty: I can . . . trust God with the results of my efforts.

1. What do you do emotionally with loved ones and friends who've died and you don't know "where they are"? From what can you draw comfort?
2. Is there anything you would do differently if you had the opportunity to repeat "light-style" evangelism in a certain relationship?
3. Who do you know who is headed for a "black hole" right now? Are there any steps God might be leading you to take?

Chapter Twenty-One: I can . . . leave a legacy of light.

1. None of us knows how far away from death we really are. What does the story of John Todd evoke in you regarding the legacy you want to leave?

2. What steps can you begin to take today to get past the *I can'ts* and grab on to the *I cans* in sharing your faith?
3. What has been the most helpful insight you've gained from reading this book?

Twinkle Resources

Know Why You Believe by Paul Little (InterVarsity)

Who Made God? by Ravi Zacharias and Norman Geisler (Zondervan)

Epic by John Eldredge (Thomas Nelson)

Telling Your Story by Toben and Joanne Heim (NavPress)

The Younger Evangelicals by Robert Webber (Baker)

The Emerging Church by Dan Kimball (Zondervan)

A New Kind of Christian by Brian McLaren (Jossey-Bass)

Character Witness by Christine Wood (InterVarsity)

Irresistible Evangelism by Steve Sjogren, Dave Ping, and Doug Pollock (Group Publishing)

Stop Witnessing and Start Loving by Paul Borthwick (NavPress)

REACH by Scott G. Wilkins (Baker)

The Celtic Way of Evangelism by George G. Hunter III (Abingdon)

Evangelism Outside the Box by Rick Richardson (InterVarsity)

Blue Like Jazz by Don Miller (Thomas Nelson)

Searching for God Knows What by Don Miller (Thomas Nelson)

Girl Meets God by Lauren Winner (Shaw)

The Coffeehouse Gospel by Matthew Paul Turner (Relevant)

From MOPS International:

Mommy Dreams (International Bible Society)

The Gift of Hope for Moms (International Bible Society)

Bible Basics 101 (MOPS International)

Mom Stars . . .
A Little Light Goes a Long Way.

If there is light in the soul,
There will be beauty in the person.
If there is beauty in the person,
There will be harmony in the house.
If there is harmony in the house,
There will be order in the nation.
If there is order in the nation,
There will be peace in the world.

Chinese Proverb

Christina tucked her knees up to shield herself from the splashes. The neighborhood pool was crowded that morning, and her territory—the wading pool—was overrun with toddlers guarded by watchful moms. It was good to get out from the apartment. With Daryl both working and going to school, the two-bedroom unit had become suffocating.

Ten-month-old Bethany sat on the top step by her mother, pouring water out of a cup, drinking more than she released. Christina rearranged the baby and sighed. She wasn't sure she liked motherhood. In New York City, her life had been full of jobs and opportunities for acting. Here in

Denver, she knew no one. Even when Daryl was home, Christina could feel his distraction. They'd both come from backgrounds of brokenness: broken marriages, past abuse, lousy families.

Stacey looked up over the wiggling bodies of her three little girls, at Christina and Bethany. Ever the baby lover, Stacey's oldest daughter picked up Bethany's cup and started to entertain her. Stacey knew well the bored look on Christina's face and suspected what lay beneath the boredom: frustration, loneliness, and wonderings of *What happened to me?*

Stacey scooted closer, began a conversation, and told her about MOPS—a group where moms of preschoolers gathered to encourage each other and learn about mothering. Before leaving the pool that day, Stacey left a card with all the specifics by Christina's towel. She wondered if she'd see Christina there or not. But sure enough, when Christina gathered Bethany up from the water and wrapped her in her alligator towel, she slid the card into the diaper bag and took it home with her.

At home, Daryl unpacked the wet contents of the pool bag and came across the card. "What's this?" he asked Christina. She told Daryl about Stacey and the group, and before she could refuse, he announced that he'd drop her off at the meeting on his way to school. It took his insistence to get her out of the car a few days later. (It's funny how shyness and inertia set in, paralyzing us in our discomfort.) Daryl unbuckled Bethany from her car seat, gathered up the diaper bag, and practically dragged Christina from the car. His firm hand on her back, nudging her forward toward the door of the building, was the last thing she remembered before making her way inside.

Christina looked across the foyer through the gathering of women she didn't know and spied Stacey. Eyes widening, Stacey bounded over and showed Christina toward the nursery where the MOPPETS program was already under way, then walked with her back to the larger room where some forty moms had arranged themselves at round tables with coffee and muffins. Within minutes, Christina found herself seated with a group of moms, answering their questions, laughing good-naturedly in response to their own awkward arrivals—dragging baby paraphernalia and grumpy children.

Eventually, Christina and Daryl started attending the church where the MOPS group met. They found Jesus . . . and some of the holes in their spirits, the broken places, began to heal. A few years later, they decided they wanted to renew their wedding vows on their tenth anniversary because they wanted to be married before God. With two more children in their family, they now welcomed Jesus into the very middle of their little unit.

It all started with a simple invitation by someone who was prepared to share starlight in another's dark season of life. A mom star shining her light before another.

We move through life—all of us—season to season. Some seasons have more darkness than others, increasing our desire for light. The journey into motherhood is such a season.

If you're a mom, you know what I mean. If you know a mom, you might know as well. If you're not . . . well, think about this: one minute your life is pretty much all about you, or all up to you. The next minute (after delivery or adoption), your life is not your own. A bundle of seven pounds commands your sleep, your body, and your brain. You have no life of your own anymore, and you won't for some time to come.

Then your identity is invaded. You used to be woman. Now you're mom. Being mom is wonderful, but it's very different from woman. Perhaps the transition from woman to wife went smoothly for you. Perhaps you skipped that stage. But moving from woman to mom is even more of an adjustment when it comes to labeling who we are.

And then there's the loneliness, the confusion, and the lack of knowing-how-to-do-this-thing-called-mothering. Okay, the season isn't DARK like cancer or terrorism or death. Sparkling moments like first steps and sticky hugs illuminate certain days. But overall, it can be pretty dim, and in the dimness, it's easy to lose your way or realize that you never knew where the way went anyway. Into this season comes a piercing need for a stable source of light. Sure, pure, clear, this-is-the-way-walk-in-it light.

It's funny how this happens. Most moms grow concerned about darkness and their need for hope out of their desire to provide this vital life ingredient for their children. Moms want to be the best moms possible. In the middle of the night, in the midst of diapering, while feeding a hungry baby, moms wonder how to nurture and train and love and help this new little life grow to its potential. And then in a moment of inadequacy—many more moments of inadequacy—moms realize that all they have to depend on is the "Me" in MomMe. That's pretty scary because most moms don't feel like there's quite enough of "Me." And in the darkness of this realization comes a pull toward something more, something outside of "Me," something more permanent, more hopeful, and brighter.

In Isaiah 40:11, God gives a picture of his connection to moms. Specifically aimed at the season of life when a woman becomes a mother and enters the "not enough of Me" moments, God walks beside us. "He tends his flock like a shepherd: He gathers the lambs in his arms and carries them close to his heart; he gently leads those that have young."

Okay, it's a shepherding metaphor, and we've been talking about light in darkness, but don't miss the point. God loves mothers. He *gets* them. And he wants to walk beside us. Bottom-line, twenty-first-century translation here is: "Don't do motherhood alone."

So, if you're a mom, *you can* be a mom star and offer light in the sometimes-dark season of motherhood, a time when a woman comes quickly to the end of herself and to the beginning of something else.

How?

Identify whom you know who's mothering today—especially those who are new at the task. You don't have to be a mom to do this. Moms who need Jesus are all around you! Just look up and down your street or apartment complex. Glance down the row at church. Take a second to notice the checkout line next to you at the market or the parents of other kids playing in the park. Pick a mom or two.

Then identify which *I can'ts* hold you back from sharing your faith. Get honest. Take the steam out of them. Go back and re-read the ones that truly hold you back.

And then identify which *I cans* you might apply to the moms you know. For sure *I can be a friend* and *I can be real* and *I can offer help in crisis*, but probably after taking another look at all the *I cans*, most of them will somehow apply to being a mom star. Grab on to the *I cans* and get glowing.

MOPS can help. The whole point of MOPS is relational evangelism. Way back in 1973, with a group of moms who were passionate about loving their neighbors with Jesus' love, MOPS began, and its approach of providing a safe and accepting place to explore motherhood and faith continues today. See, there are a few seasons in life when we're *most* open to the hope God offers. As children, as teens when we're forming an identity, when we face a crisis or are at death's door, and when we become parents. Into this season of parenting comes MOPS with a felt-need approach to mothering and faith. Over the past several decades, the goal of the MOPS ministry has been to bring each mom—and her family—one step closer to Jesus.

On the fringes of your life is a Christina, with a Daryl and a Bethany who need the light of Jesus. They're facing a season when the direction of their lives will be formed, their values and goals determined, and the way they live shaped. Be a mom star. Shine the light of Jesus around them that they might see the source of the hope they seek and choose well the way they will walk in.

"He tends his flock like a shepherd: He gathers the lambs in his arms and carries them close to his heart; he gently leads those that have young."
. . . .
Isaiah 40:11

About MOPS

You take care of your children, Mom. Who takes care of you? MOPS® International (Mothers of Preschoolers) provides mothers of preschoolers with the nurture and resources they need to be the best moms they can be.

MOPS is dedicated to the message that "mothering matters" and that moms of young children need encouragement during these critical and formative years. Chartered groups meet in approximately four thousand churches and Christian ministries throughout the United States and in thirty other countries. Each MOPS program helps mothers find friendship and acceptance, provides opportunities for women to develop and practice leadership skills in the group, and promotes spiritual growth. MOPS groups are chartered ministries of local churches and meet at a variety of times and locations: daytime, evenings, and on weekends; in churches, homes, and workplaces.

The MOPPETS program offers a loving, learning experience for children while their moms attend MOPS. Other MOPS resources include *MOMSense®* magazine and radio, the MOPS International website, and books and resources available through the MOPShop.

There are 14.3 million mothers of preschoolers in the United States alone, and many moms can't attend a local MOPS group. These moms still need the support that MOPS International can offer! For a small registration fee, any mother of preschoolers can join the MOPS♥to♥Mom Connection® and receive *MOMSense* magazine six times a year, a weekly Mom-E-Mail message of encouragement, and other valuable benefits.

Find out how MOPS International can help you become part of the MOPS♥to♥Mom Connection and/or join or start a MOPS group. Visit our website at www.MOPS.org. Phone us at 303-733-5353. Or email Info@MOPS.org. To learn how to start a MOPS group, call 1-888-910-MOPS.

Elisa Morgan is president and CEO of MOPS International, Inc. (www. MOPS.org), based in Denver, Colorado. Her daily radio program, *MOMSense*, is broadcast on more than seven hundred outlets nationwide. She is the author of *Naked Fruit*, *The Orchard*, *Mom to Mom*, and *Meditations for Mothers*; editor of *Mom's Devotional Bible*, *Mom, You Make a Difference!*, and *God's Words of Life for Moms*; and coauthor of *What Every Child Needs*, *What Every Mom Needs*, *Children Change a Marriage*, *Make Room for Daddy*, and *Real Moms*. Elisa and her husband, Evan, live with their family in Centennial, Colorado.

Twinkle

By Jane Taylor
1806

Twinkle, twinkle, little star,
How I wonder what you are.
Up above the world so high,
Like a diamond in the sky.

When the blazing sun is gone,
When he nothing shines upon,
Then you show your little light,
Twinkle, twinkle all the night.

Twinkle, twinkle, little star,
How I wonder what you are.

Then the traveler in the dark,
Thanks you for your tiny spark.
She could not see where to go,
If you did not twinkle so. . . .

Twinkle, twinkle, little star,
How I wonder what you are.

In the dark blue sky you keep,
Often through my curtains peep.
For you never shut your eye,
Till the sun is in the sky.

Twinkle, twinkle, little star,
How I wonder what you are.

A modern-day
parable of God's
faithfulness

Booklets sold in packs of 10

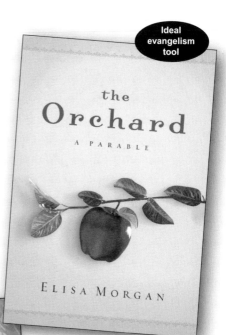

Ideal evangelism tool

the
Orchard
A PARABLE

ELISA MORGAN

Grow by expressing
your God-given
personality

naked fruit

>>elisa morgan